P9-EES-762

PRODUCTIVITY POLICY:
Key to the Nation's Economic Future

A Statement by the Research and
Policy Committee of the
Committee for Economic Development

April 1983

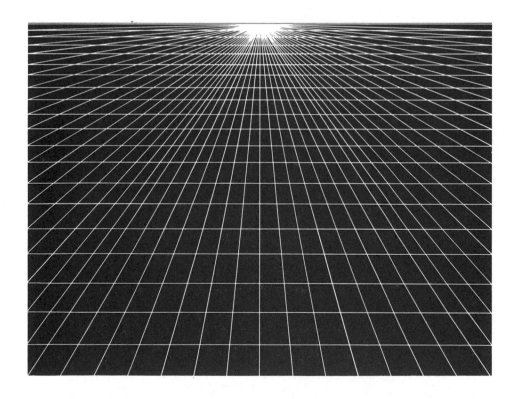

Library of Congress Cataloging in Publication Data

Committee for Economic Development. Research and
    Policy Committee.
    Productivity policy.

    "April 1983."
    Includes bibliographical references.
    1. Industrial productivity—United States.
2. Industrial productivity.   I. Title.
HC110.I52C65 1983   338'.06'0973   83–1873
ISBN 0-87186-776-1 (lib. bdg.)
ISBN 0-87186-076-7 (pbk.)

First printing: April 1983
Paperback: $8.50
Library binding: $10.50
Printed in the United States of America
Design: Stead Young & Rowe Inc

COMMITTEE FOR ECONOMIC DEVELOPMENT
477 Madison Avenue, New York, N.Y. 10022
1700 K Street N.W., Washington, D.C. 20006

CONTENTS

RESPONSIBILITY FOR CED STATEMENTS ON NATIONAL POLICY   vi

PURPOSE OF THIS STATEMENT   ix

1. INTRODUCTION AND SUMMARY OF RECOMMENDATIONS   1
Summary of Major Recommendations   5

2. WHAT IS PRODUCTIVITY? MEASUREMENT AND
SIGNIFICANCE OF THE PROBLEM   8
On the Meaning and Measurement of Productivity   9
How Serious the Slowdown?   12
U.S. and Foreign Productivity Performance   12
Toward Policy: General Considerations   18
Causes and Remedies   22

3. WHY WORRY ABOUT PRODUCTIVITY?   23
Productivity and International Competitive Position   27

4. ON THE CAUSES OF THE PRODUCTIVITY SLOWDOWN   30
Capital Formation   32
Research and Development Outlays   34
Composition of Output   36
Composition of the Labor Force   37
Energy Prices and Natural Resources   37
Government Regulation   38
Business Fluctuations   40
Evaluating the Statistical Indicators   40
Other Impediments to Productivity Growth   40
Product Quality as a Component of Productivity   42

5. PUBLIC POLICIES FOR PRODUCTIVITY GROWTH   45
Increased Investment: The Price of Growth   45
Stimulating Saving and Investment   48
Directing Investment toward Opportunities for Productivity Growth   53
Stimulating Technological Change   57
Removing Unnecessary Regulatory Impediments   63
Reducing the Cost of Regulatory Goals   65
Federal Research and Technology-Enhancing Programs   68
The Complex Business-Government Relationship   69

168495

EMORY & HENRY LIBRARY

6. WHAT MANAGEMENT AND LABOR CAN DO   71
Strategic Tools for Productivity Growth   72
Formulating Operational Productivity Goals   75
Entrepreneurship: The Basis for Achieving Productivity Goals   76
Choosing a Portfolio of Productivity-Stimulating Techniques   78
Operational Techniques to Improve Productivity   80
Labor-Management Participation Teams   85
Productivity-Training Programs   86
Employment Tenure   87
Management Incentives   88
Concluding Comments   91

MEMORANDA OF COMMENT, RESERVATION, OR DISSENT   93

APPENDIX: SUCCESSFUL ECONOMIC POLICY IN THE FAR EAST   95
Labor Relations   97
Consumer Credit, Pension, and Housing Arrangements   99
Taxation and Saving   101
Government-Directed Investment   102
Taxation of Business and Capital Gains   104
Conclusions   106

OBJECTIVES OF THE COMMITTEE FOR ECONOMIC DEVELOPMENT   108

PRODUCTIVITY POLICY:
Key to the Nation's
Economic Future

RESPONSIBILITY FOR CED STATEMENTS ON NATIONAL POLICY

The Committee for Economic Development is an independent research and educational organization of two hundred business executives and educators. CED is nonprofit, nonpartisan, and nonpolitical. Its purpose is to propose policies that will help to bring about steady economic growth at high employment and reasonably stable prices, increase productivity and living standards, provide greater and more equal opportunity for every citizen, and improve the quality of life for all. A more complete description of CED appears on page 108.

All CED policy recommendations must have the approval of trustees on the Research and Policy Committee. This committee is directed under the bylaws to "initiate studies into the principles of business policy and of public policy which will foster the full contribution by industry and commerce to the attainment and maintenance" of the objectives stated above. The bylaws emphasize that "all research is to be thoroughly objective in character, and the approach in each instance is to be from the standpoint of the general welfare and not from that of any special political or economic group." The committee is aided by a Research Advisory Board of leading social scientists and by a small permanent professional staff.

The Research and Policy Committee does not attempt to pass judgment on any pending specific legislative proposals; its purpose is to urge careful consideration of the objectives set forth in this statement and of the best means of accomplishing those objectives.

Each statement is preceded by extensive discussions, meetings, and exchange of memoranda. The research is undertaken by a subcommittee, assisted by advisors chosen for their competence in the field under study. The members and advisors of the subcommittee that prepared this statement are listed on page viii.

The full Research and Policy Committee participates in the drafting of recommendations. Likewise, the trustees on the drafting subcommittee vote to approve or disapprove a policy statement, and they share with the Research and Policy Committee the privilege of submitting individual comments for publication, as noted on pages 93 and 94 and on the appropriate page of the text of the statement.

Except for the members of the Research and Policy Committee and the responsible subcommittee, the recommendations presented herein are not necessarily endorsed by other trustees or by the advisors, contributors, staff members, or others associated with CED.

RESEARCH AND POLICY COMMITTEE

Chairman
WILLIAM F. MAY

Vice Chairmen
WILLIAM S. EDGERLY/*Education and Social and Urban Development*
EDMUND B. FITZGERALD/*International Economy*
RODERICK M. HILLS/*Improvement of Management in Government*
ROCCO C. SICILIANO/*National Economy*

A. ROBERT ABBOUD, President
Occidental Petroleum Corporation

RAND V. ARASKOG, Chairman
and President
ITT Corporation

*ROY L. ASH
Los Angeles, California

JOSEPH W. BARR, Corporate
Director
Arlington, Virginia

HARRY HOOD BASSETT, Chairman,
Executive Committee
Southeast Bank N.A.

ROBERT A. BECK, Chairman
The Prudential Insurance
Company of America

JACK F. BENNETT, Senior Vice
President
Exxon Corporation

OWEN B. BUTLER, Chairman
The Procter & Gamble Company

FLETCHER L. BYROM, Retired Chairman
Koppers Company, Inc.

ROBERT J. CARLSON
Executive Vice President–Power
United Technologies Corporation

*RAFAEL CARRION, JR., Chairman
Banco Popular de Puerto Rico

WILLIAM S. CASHEL, JR.
Vice Chairman
American Telephone
and Telegraph Company

JOHN B. CAVE, Executive Vice President
and Chief Financial Officer
McGraw-Hill, Inc.

EMILIO G. COLLADO, Chairman
Grace Geothermal Corporation

RICHARD M. CYERT, President
Carnegie-Mellon University

D. RONALD DANIEL, Managing Director
McKinsey & Company, Inc.

JOHN H. DANIELS, Retired
Chairman
National City Bancorporation

W. D. EBERLE, President
Manchester Associates, Ltd.

WILLIAM S. EDGERLY, Chairman
and President
State Street Bank and Trust Company

THOMAS J. EYERMAN, Partner
Skidmore, Owings & Merrill

FRANCIS E. FERGUSON, Chairman
Northwestern Mutual Life
Insurance Company

JOHN H. FILER, Chairman
Aetna Life and Casualty Company

WILLIAM S. FISHMAN, Chairman
ARA Services, Inc.

EDMUND B. FITZGERALD, President
Northern Telecom Limited

WILLIAM C. GREENOUGH, Retired
Chairman
TIAA and CREF

PHILIP M. HAWLEY, President
Carter Hawley Hale Stores, Inc.

RODERICK M. HILLS, Chairman
Sears World Trade, Inc.

ROBERT C. HOLLAND, President
Committee for Economic Development

JAMES L. KETELSEN, Chairman
Tenneco Inc.

*PHILIP M. KLUTZNICK, Senior Partner
Klutznick Investments

RALPH LAZARUS, Chairman,
Executive Committee
Federated Department Stores, Inc.

*FRANKLIN A. LINDSAY, Chairman,
Executive Committee
Itek Corporation

J. PAUL LYET, Former Chairman
Sperry Corporation

G. BARRON MALLORY
New York, New York

WILLIAM F. MAY, Dean
New York University Graduate
School of Business Administration

ALONZO L. McDONALD, Consultant
Bloomfield Hills, Michigan

JAMES W. McKEE, JR., Chairman
CPC International Inc.

E. L. McNEELY
La Jolla, California

*J. W. McSWINEY, Director
The Mead Corporation

RUBEN F. METTLER, Chairman
TRW Inc.

STEVEN MULLER, President
The Johns Hopkins University

NORMA PACE, Senior Vice President
American Paper Institute

VICTOR H. PALMIERI, Chairman
Victor Palmieri
and Company Incorporated

C. WREDE PETERSMEYER
Vero Beach, Florida

R. STEWART RAUCH, Chairman,
Executive Committee
General Accident Insurance Companies

JAMES Q. RIORDAN, Executive
Vice President
Mobil Corporation

HENRY B. SCHACHT, Chairman
Cummins Engine Company, Inc.

RICHARD R. SHINN, Former Chairman
Metropolitan Life Insurance
Company

ROCCO C. SICILIANO, Chairman
Ticor

*RICHARD M. SMITH, Vice Chairman
Bethlehem Steel Corporation

ROGER B. SMITH, Chairman
General Motors Corporation

*ELMER B. STAATS, Former Comptroller
General of the United States
Washington, D.C.

CHARLES B. STAUFFACHER
Financial Consultant
Universe Tank Ships, Inc.

WILLIAM C. STOLK
Easton, Connecticut

WILLIS A. STRAUSS, Chairman
InterNorth, Inc.

WALTER N. THAYER, Chairman
Whitney Communications Corporation

W. BRUCE THOMAS
Vice Chairman of Administration
and Chief Financial Officer
United States Steel Corporation

SIDNEY J. WEINBERG, JR., Partner
Goldman, Sachs & Co.

JOHN F. WELCH, JR., Chairman
General Electric Company

ALTON W. WHITEHOUSE, JR., Chairman
Standard Oil Company (Ohio)

FRAZAR B. WILDE, Chairman Emeritus
Connecticut General Life
Insurance Company

RICHARD D. WOOD, Chairman and
President
Eli Lilly and Company

*Voted to approve the policy statement but submitted memoranda of comment, reservation, or dissent.

SUBCOMMITTEE ON PRODUCTIVITY

Chairman
WILLIAM F. MAY
Dean
New York University
   Graduate School
   of Business Administration

Vice Chairman
EDMUND T. PRATT, JR.
Chairman
Pfizer Inc.

JACK F. BENNETT
Senior Vice President
Exxon Corporation

ALAN S. BOYD
President
Airbus Industrie of
   North America

OWEN B. BUTLER
Chairman
The Procter & Gamble Company

ROBERT J. CARLSON
Executive Vice President—Power
United Technologies Corporation

WILLIAM S. CASHEL, JR.
Vice Chairman
American Telephone and
   Telegraph Company

DAVID R. CLARE
President
Johnson & Johnson

RALPH P. DAVIDSON
Chairman
Time Inc.

PETER A. DEROW
President
CBS/Publishing Group

JOHN R. EDMAN
Vice President
General Motors Corporation

JAMES B. FARLEY
Chairman
Booz·Allen & Hamilton Inc.

WILLIAM S. FISHMAN
Chairman
ARA Services, Inc.

DONALD E. GARRETSON
Vice President, Finance
3M Company

W. H. KROME GEORGE
Chairman
Aluminum Company of America

THOMAS C. GRAHAM
President
Jones & Laughlin Steel
   Corporation

LAWRENCE HICKEY
Chairman
Stein Roe & Farnham

E. ROBERT KINNEY
President
Investors Group of Companies

FRANKLIN A. LINDSAY
Chairman, Executive Committee
Itek Corporation

GEORGE M. LOW
President
Rensselaer Polytechnic Institute

ALONZO L. McDONALD
Consultant
Bloomfield Hills, Michigan

NORMA PACE
Senior Vice President
American Paper Institute

C. WREDE PETERSMEYER
Vero Beach, Florida

PETER G. PETERSON
Chairman and President
Lehman Brothers Kuhn Loeb, Inc.

DEAN P. PHYPERS
Senior Vice President
IBM Corporation

DONALD B. SMILEY
Chairman, Finance Committee
R. H. Macy & Co., Inc.

RICHARD M. SMITH
Vice Chairman
Bethlehem Steel Corporation

ELMER B. STAATS
Former Comptroller General
   of the United States
Washington, D.C.

L. STANTON WILLIAMS
Chairman
PPG Industries, Inc.

Nontrustee Members*

ROBERT KURTZ
Retired Senior Vice President
   of Corporate Production
   and Operations
General Electric Company

JOHN STEWART
Director
McKinsey & Company, Inc.

W. J. USERY, JR.
Bill Usery Associates

*Nontrustee members take part in all discussions of the statement but do not vote on it.

OTHER TRUSTEES AND ADVISORS

FRANK N. BARCH
Manager, Industrial
   Engineering
ITT Corporation

MARTIN BRONFENBRENNER
Kenan Professor of Economics
Duke University

ALAN K. CAMPBELL
Executive Vice President,
   Management & Public Affairs
ARA Services, Inc.

FRANK GOLLOP
Professor of Economics
Boston College

GORDON C. HURLBERT
President—Power Systems Company
Westinghouse Electric Corporation

JAN KLEIN
Sloan School of Management
Massachusetts Institute
   of Technology

GEORGE H. KUPER
Wilton, Connecticut

EDWIN MANSFIELD
Professor of Economics
University of Pennsylvania

ROBERT B. McKERSIE
Professor, Sloan School
   of Management
Massachusetts Institute
   of Technology

ROBERT E. MERRIAM
Partner
Alexander Proudfoot Company

JACK A. MEYER
Resident Fellow in Economics
American Enterprise Institute

RICHARD W. MOONEY
Vice President—Productivity
   Improvement
GTE Corporation

JOHN R. NORSWORTHY
Chief, Center for Economic Studies
Bureau of the Census

GEORGE SADLER
Senior Economist
American Productivity Center

THOMAS C. SCHELLING
Professor of Political Economy
John Fitzgerald Kennedy
   School of Government
Harvard University

FRANK W. SCHIFF
Vice President and Chief Economist
Committee for Economic Development

ELEANOR C. THOMAS
Policy Analyst, Division of Policy
   Research and Analysis
National Science Foundation

CARL G. THOR
Vice President
American Productivity Center

HOWARD S. TURNER
Retired Chairman of the Board
Turner Construction Company

BRIAN L. USILANER
Associate Director
General Accounting Office

EDWARD WOLFF
Associate Professor of Economics
New York University

PROJECT DIRECTOR

WILLIAM J. BAUMOL
Professor of Economics
Princeton University and New York University

STAFF COUNSELOR

KENNETH McLENNAN
Vice President and Director of
   Industrial Studies
Committee for Economic Development

PROJECT STAFF

SUE ANNE BATEY BLACKMAN
Princeton University

PATRICIA BUCKLEY FREDERICK
Policy Analyst
Committee for Economic Development

LORRAINE M. BROOKER
Administrative Assistant
Committee for Economic Development

SEONG H. PARK
Economist
Committee for Economic Development

MARGARET J. HERRE
Assistant Director, Business-Government
   Relations and Assistant Secretary,
   Research and Policy Committee
Committee for Economic Development

PROJECT EDITOR

CLAUDIA P. FEUREY
Director of Information
Committee for Economic Development

PURPOSE OF THIS STATEMENT

Among business and labor leaders, government officials, and the general public, there has been a growing awareness both of the critical importance of improving productivity in the U.S. economy and the serious threat posed by the nation's lagging productivity rate. For a number of years, the American economy has trailed badly behind other industrialized economies in productivity-growth rates. In some industries, in some years, productivity has actually declined. Already the economy is feeling the effects of this inability to keep up, with many industries finding it difficult to retain their share of foreign markets and others facing stiffer competition at home from foreign-produced goods.

When the trustees of CED undertook this project, we were aware that while much had been written on productivity, the contradictions in academic research findings, the confusions of definitions, the conflicts in recommended solutions, and the troublesome tendency to focus on short-term measures were actually inhibiting our ability to form coherent, workable public and private policies.

As a business-academic organization we were also keenly aware that the diverging views among academic researchers and public and private policy makers were leading to a general misunderstanding of the serious implications of a continued slowdown in U.S. productivity growth. A key message of this report is that unless the United States is able to achieve and maintain a productivity-growth rate comparable to the rates of other industrial nations, U.S. firms—in almost all sectors of the economy—will find it increasingly difficult to compete in world markets. This will mean the loss of market share for some companies and industries, and loss of jobs for American workers. In addition, if productivity is not substantially improved over the long term, this nation faces the very real prospects of reduced standards of living for *all* its citizens and of a threatened national security.

FUNDAMENTAL CHANGES

Thoughtful, innovative, and long-range actions by business, government, and labor are needed and needed now. Further, it is important for all who take action to understand that half-hearted, piecemeal measures will simply not be effective in raising U.S. productivity to a level where American products and workers are competitive with their high levels of real wages. What this policy statement emphasizes—and what I believe to be its great strength—is that long-term, and in some cases, fundamental changes are needed in management and labor practices, in laws, and in public policies to release again the competitive energies of American business and workers.

For this report we drew extensively on recent CED policy statements, which also have stressed the interconnecting nature of social and economic problems. Particularly pertinent were *Stimulating Technological Progress* (1980), *Fighting Inflation and Rebuilding a Sound Economy* (1980), and *Redefining Government's Role in the Market System* (1979).

SPECIAL CONTRIBUTIONS

I wish to acknowledge the contributions of the extraordinarily able business and academic leaders who served on the subcommittee and the advisors and CED staff who assisted in the preparation of this report. A list of their names appears on page viii. In addition, I particularly wish to thank William J. Baumol, professor of economics at New York and Princeton Universities, and project counselor Kenneth McLennan, vice president for industrial studies for CED, for their insightful approach to this difficult issue.

As chairman of the subcommittee that prepared this report, and now as the new chairman of the CED Research and Policy Committee, I have had the special honor of observing this talented group at work and of guiding the report's growth and development.

Finally, I wish to give special thanks to the Alfred P. Sloan Foundation for the generous support that made this project possible.

William F. May
Chairman
Research and Policy Committee

CHAPTER 1

INTRODUCTION AND
SUMMARY OF RECOMMENDATIONS

Increased productivity is the key to economic progress. It allows the nation to raise its standard of living, to support such social goals as education and health care, and to contribute to other aspects of the general welfare; it is an essential underpinning of the nation's security. Higher productivity allows these "noneconomic" objectives to be achieved without absolute reduction of workers' living standards. Moreover, productivity growth offers intangible rewards through its contribution to national morale. A nation whose productivity is declining is likely to be beset by doubts and a decline in self-confidence as well as in material well-being.

Although the achievement of some national objectives depends solely on America's own growth rate, other goals depend on the relation between the U.S. growth rate and those of other countries. For example, the purchasing power of the wages earned by American workers is affected primarily by the U.S. productivity level. In many U.S. industries, the level of productivity is probably still somewhat higher than it is in other industrialized countries. However, if the average U.S. worker's real wage is to grow commensurately with average real wages in other industrialized countries, growth in output per worker has to expand, not fall behind that in other economies.

The brisk upturn in productivity in 1982 should not lull us into a false sense of security. While more U.S. businesses are now giving high priority to productivity improvement, most of the recent increase is probably a temporary phenomenon that can be expected during the early stages of an economic recovery. A continuation of the decline in the U.S. productivity-growth rate during the 1970s is still cause for serious concern. We should be equally disturbed by the facts that for several decades a number of other industrialized countries have surpassed us significantly in the rate of improvement, and that in a number of industries, this nation has lost its competitiveness in world markets.

Proposals for increased productivity growth must be judged in terms of probable costs and benefits, just as the proposed elements of any national policy would be. Few (if any) policies are entirely cost-free. The need to evaluate costs and benefits is underscored by the belief that growth is only an instrument for the promotion of economic and social goals, not an ultimate objective. A firm resolve to reject all bitter medicine out of hand may preclude many measures that promise to be effective. Nor is there any basis for the comforting belief that substantial improvements can be achieved by routine measures.

Recognizing that no productivity program can be expected to provide overnight miracles, our recommendations are oriented deliberately toward the long run, seeking lasting stimulation of productivity growth rather than effects that are largely transitory. In the long run, productivity improvement is inextricably tied to private enterprise, the driving force of which, entrepreneurship, provides the willingness to venture onto uncharted paths. The entrepreneurial spirit may yet prove to be as important for growth policy as it is for growth itself.

Even though some command economies have achieved significant short-run rates of growth, not one of the world's leaders in productivity levels—now or in the past—has been a centrally directed economy or one in which industry is predominantly nationalized. It is true that several of the economies whose productivity has increased most rapidly in recent years are characterized by varying degrees of government intervention and lack of political freedom, but each of these countries ultimately relies on the market mechanism.

An effective program for the stimulation of productivity will have to deal with a number of crucial issues. Our policy recommendations focus on six of these.*

- ● Removal of impediments to saving and to investment in business activity to raise them to levels compatible with our economy and commensurate with those in the countries that are ahead of us in productivity-growth rates.

---

*See memorandum by Roy L. Ash, page 93.

- Federal support for basic research to preserve U.S. technological leadership.

- Reduction of unnecessary and inefficient regulatory constraints on the productivity performance of labor and management personnel.

- Reduction of inhibitions to movement of capital, labor, and other resources toward the most promising prospects for productivity growth and away from activities in which such opportunities have declined, except where such industries are essential to national security and public welfare.

- Creation of a climate that encourages entrepreneurial initiative for increased productivity.

- Restructuring of labor-management relationships, with particular attention to incentives for increased cooperation between labor and management personnel for educating, understanding, and communicating the need for productivity improvement and cooperation in adapting to technological innovation and other forms of change.

Neglect of any of these issues may seriously weaken the effectiveness of any proposed program. The U.S. economy clearly cannot keep up if its capital stock is inadequate or obsolete, if it falls behind technologically, if its labor force resists every measure to increase productivity, if industry decision making is constrained at every turn, if capital does not flow in the directions in which it can do the most good, or if management turns in an inadequate performance. On the other hand, a program that promises to bring significant progress on each of these fronts is indeed likely to move us a long way toward attaining our national goals.

However, even such a program will not be sufficient to attain these goals unless effective action is also taken in a number of other areas. In this policy statement, we make no specific policy recommendations on these other elements of an overall program for the stimulation of productivity growth because we have dealt with them in previous statements or plan to discuss them in future publications. These elements include:

- the role of fiscal, monetary, and other broad national policies in achieving noninflationary economic growth;[1]

---

1. See the policy statement *Fighting Inflation and Rebuilding a Sound Economy* (New York: CED, 1980); and Fletcher L. Byrom, testimony on the State of the Economy before the Joint Economic Committee (97th Congress, 2nd session, 2 April 1982).

4

- an appropriate level of investment in human capital to equip the labor force with the education, skills, and adaptability needed to meet the requirements of the coming decade.

A recent CED policy statement presents detailed recommendations for increased cooperation between the public and private sectors to improve the training and employability of the hard-to-employ.[2] But more needs to be done to improve the U.S. educational system so that in the future the work force will be better able to adapt to structural changes in the economy. One area of special concern from the viewpoint of productivity is the need to ensure an adequate supply of highly skilled workers such as scientists and engineers.[3]

There are no instant cures for poor productivity performance; measures intended to make a difference overnight are likely to prove ineffective or short-lived. It is therefore essential that we begin, without delay and before the full social costs of the productivity-growth slowdown have occurred, to design and institute measures that really do promise to deal with the problem effectively. Once such a program is under way, we must exercise patience, recognizing that sufficient time must be allowed for the benefits to emerge. Here, as in any area of public policy, it is essential that the long view prevail and that the nation be prepared to take whatever bold steps are required today to assure its future well-being.

It is encouraging that in recent years the productivity problem has begun to receive recognition by the general public and that the first steps have been taken toward the analysis of appropriate policy. The recent establishment of the National Productivity Advisory Committee by the President is significant, although the Committee's predecessors were permitted to lapse. There has been considerable growth in the number of corporations that have appointed senior officials whose task is the improvement of productivity. And there are now more than forty centers in the United States at universities and elsewhere devoted to the study of this problem. Important changes in labor and management attitudes toward productivity-improving measures also appear to be taking place in some businesses. The task now is to make the most of these promising beginnings.

---

2. See the policy statement *Jobs for the Hard-to-Employ: New Directions for a Public-Private Partnership* (New York: CED, 1978); the program statement *Employment Policy for the Hard-to-Employ: The Path of Progress* (New York: CED, 1982); and Franklin A. Lindsay, testimony on Human Investment Policy before the House Committee on the Budget (97th Congress, 2nd session, 15 March 1982).

---

3. Two forthcoming CED policy statements, one on Industrial Strategy and Trade Policy and another on Business and the Schools, will include more extensive discussions of investment in human capital.

SUMMARY OF MAJOR RECOMMENDATIONS

In this statement we discuss what government and the private sector can do to improve productivity. For government, our major public-policy recommendations include eliminating unnecessary government constraints on the market system and the modification of policies that discourage sorely needed saving and investment.

Tax and other policies must remove gradually the bias in favor of current consumption and encourage higher rates of saving and investment. The consumption bias in public expenditures, which has favored social transfers, should also be curtailed and emphasis instead placed on shifting investment toward such public infrastructure as roads, bridges, and harbors that will contribute to greater productivity in the entire economy.

To encourage saving and investment, the statement also recommends:

- adoption of some mechanism to adjust the valuation of capital gains for inflation;

- deferring taxation of employee contributions to retirement plans (Social Security and employer plans) from the time employee income is earned to the time retirement benefits are received.

In the interest of stimulating saving and investment by individuals, the report also recommends future consideration of simplifying the current tax code by broadening the tax base and reducing marginal tax rates. Lower marginal tax rates will encourage greater labor-force participation and increase the incentive for individuals to save. It is also important to move toward a tax system that is as neutral as possible in the taxation of income from different capital assets. This Committee strongly supports the recent reduction in the taxation of such income in the Economic Recovery Tax Act of 1981. We feel that "expensing," that is, immediate deductibility of business capital investment, would also reduce the cost of business capital while at the same time allow similar treatment of income from all assets. If the tax code moved toward expensing, some of the current special tax arrangements for business would no longer be necessary. This change should be considered in the future.

Government should also make basic research an important priority. We support the recent changes in tax law that encourage business to help universities acquire equipment for basic research, and we recommend a number of other steps.

6

- Government should pay the full cost of research performed under contract by universities.

- To encourage the development of high-quality researchers, government should finance individual scholars of outstanding ability rather than invest equally among a large number of institutions.

Government has a legitimate regulatory role in the economy, but unnecessary and inefficient techniques, even if used to achieve a desirable regulatory goal, will inhibit productivity growth. We therefore recommend that the government continue economic deregulation in areas in which effective competition is no longer absent. We believe that many markets served by public utilities and by the railroad, trucking, and air-transportation industries now meet this test.

In implementing regulatory policy, government should encourage wider use of the "bubble" and "offsets" concepts.

- Government should simplify and rapidly accelerate the approval process for use of the bubble and offsets programs.

- New as well as old plant and equipment should be eligible for inclusion in the bubble and the offsets programs.

- New-source performance-standard regulations, which now restrict the inclusion of new plant and equipment in the bubble, should be modified by amending the enabling legislation to permit more general use of the innovative bubble concept.

In the long run, the quality of business decisions will improve if management can spend more time on producing its output efficiently than on reacting to a complex set of economic and social regulations.

If the market system is to be effective in stimulating productivity, government cannot, and should not, intervene to protect individual firms from market forces whenever an individual firm or single industry experiences economic difficulties.

However great the importance of proper government policies, and however significant the changes in overall circumstances to which business must adapt, the critical role in productivity performance is played by business management, which makes most of the decisions regarding the country's production of goods and services.*

A large array of productivity-stimulating techniques is available to business managers.

*See memorandum by Franklin A. Lindsay, page 93.

- Recognizing that the choice of specific techniques for productivity improvement must be adapted to the needs and capabilities of the individual firm or industry, we recommend that every American business adopt *explicit productivity goals* that it considers adequate for meeting its competitive challenges now and in the future.

- Management must set productivity goals for its own organization and select the *appropriate techniques* for a successful productivity strategy. Since entrepreneurship is an important key to productivity improvement in all firms, however, it must be encouraged by top management, and promising new ideas, even if they disturb the status quo, should be nurtured within the entire organization.

- Workers have a stake in their firm's productivity performance. The experience of the most innovative firms demonstrates that employees and union leadership (in companies with unions) must be substantially involved in designing and implementing productivity-enhancing policies.

- Compensation systems that include financial incentives for improved productivity should be a common element in the employee involvement of both labor and management.

The appropriate public-policy environment, including moderate noninflationary growth, is an essential prerequisite for substantial and sustained productivity improvement. But the actions of management and labor can also contribute dramatically to the efficiency of every sector of the U.S. economy. With the restoration of appropriate incentives, and with the adoption of measures that are sufficiently bold and imaginative, we can be confident that the nation will rise to the challenge once again.

CHAPTER 2

WHAT IS PRODUCTIVITY? MEASUREMENT AND SIGNIFICANCE OF THE PROBLEM

The productivity problem involves a complex set of issues, some more serious and more intractable than others. To begin with, there are at least two different and important productivity problems.

The first is *the slowdown in the rate of productivity growth in the United States*, which began somewhere between the middle and the end of the 1960s: by the end of the 1970s, there had been several years in which productivity for the private business sector as a whole apparently did not grow at all. The second problem is *the very much lower rate of U.S. productivity growth throughout the past two decades in comparison with the rates of Japan, Italy, France, Sweden, West Germany (the Federal Republic), and other industrialized countries.*

These two problems have different implications for future economic policy. The fact that the deceleration of U.S. productivity has been paralleled by slowdowns in other countries may offer some measure of comfort about the long-run implications of the U.S. productivity decline, but it should be remembered that the nation's *competitive* position depends primarily on its *relative* level of productivity.

If the U.S. growth rate continues to lag substantially behind that of other industrialized countries, and if such differences continue for a protracted period, our relative standard of living must decline. Some American industries will find themselves at a serious competitive disadvantage. While our economy-wide productivity level is still generally high, it is obvious enough that American preeminence has already been challenged; in some critical sectors of the economy this country has already been overtaken.

ON THE MEANING AND MEASUREMENT OF PRODUCTIVITY

Productivity measures the relationship between outputs (the amounts of goods and services produced) and inputs (the quantities of labor, capital, and material resources used to produce the outputs). When the same amount of input produces larger quantities of goods and services than before, or when the same amount of output is produced with smaller quantities of inputs, productivity has increased.

In practice, measuring changes in productivity is not so simple. For example, the proportions of outputs may change over time or vary among producers, making it difficult to define the behavior of overall output. Public-service output is particularly difficult to quantify because it does not consist of a stream of products or services that have a market value. Few industries or plants produce only one product. Sometimes a single process yields more than one product. Combining these products into a single output figure requires that they be weighted by some measure of relative importance.

Total input is equally difficult to measure properly. Many inputs must be combined to produce an output, but productivity ratios often relate output to a single input, such as labor. When there is a change in a productivity ratio calculated on a single input, it is important not to attribute the change to that one input. In an interrelated economic system the change may be influenced by any or all of the multitude of variables, such as production techniques, capital equipment, the skill of the work force, managerial performance, the rate of capacity utilization, the scale of operations, materials flow, product mix, the state of labor-management relations, and the quality of the work environment. The relative importance of these influences varies from country to country, from sector to sector, and from organization to organization, as well as over time. In addition, the difficulties of measuring improvements in product quality undoubtedly cause errors in productivity-growth measures (see "Measuring Productivity," pages 10 and 11).

Unfortunately, it is impossible even to provide a single set of numbers that represents a consensus among those who have studied the deceleration in U.S. productivity. Every report makes somewhat different estimates.

Nevertheless, despite their quantitative differences, the studies are virtually unanimous in their qualitative conclusions about the magnitude and duration of the problem.

The main difficulty in trying to measure productivity growth or decline is the inherent ambiguity of the concepts involved. There simply is no single definition of the term "productivity." Consequently, there is no one correct way to measure its growth.

Future research will probably not eliminate the measurement problem. A perfect productivity index is conceptually impossible because no one

MEASURING PRODUCTIVITY

Two types of productivity measures are commonly used: *labor productivity* and *total-factor or multifactor productivity*. Labor productivity commonly measures output per hour (based on hours worked or hours paid for) in a plant, industry, or some national aggregate, such as the private sector. Total-factor productivity includes not only labor input but also the services of plant and equipment (capital), sometimes energy, and materials. When output is measured on a *value-added* basis (as in the GNP accounts), only *capital and labor inputs* are included in the total-factor productivity measure. All intermediate inputs are netted out. When output is measured as *gross output* (or *physical units* of output), all *purchased* inputs are included in the input measure. Most studies recognize labor, capital, energy, and "material" (meaning all other purchased services usually included in that category).

Each type of measure has its advantages and its limitations. In each case, the output measure includes the effects of technological changes, the improved quality of capital goods, the increasing skill and education of the labor force, and many other sources of productive efficiency not purchased directly. Total-factor productivity is appropriate when assessing the structure of production and changes in costs and prices, especially when all purchased inputs are included in the analysis; it also provides a better framework for analysis of substitution among factors of production. Even capital-labor substitution depends on the quantities of energy and materials involved in the production process. Labor productivity, on the other hand, is a more significant determinant of the nation's standard of living.

In an important sense, it is possible to have the best of both worlds. Modern methods permit us to study labor productivity in a total-factor framework. In this way, we can express labor productivity growth as deriving from growth in the ratios of capital, energy, and materials to labor, as well as the growth in overall efficiency (that is, growth in total-number can accurately describe the behavior of so many outputs, inputs, and quality variations. Fortunately, the usefulness of productivity measurement rests not on any hope of eliminating this difficulty but rather on experience that confirms that, in most cases, the different methods of productivity measurement yield entirely consistent results. [1]

1. For excellent discussions of the conceptual problems and measurement issues associated with productivity, see Albert Rees, "Improving Productivity Measurement," *American Economic Review* 70 (May 1980), 340–342, and the same author's "Improving the Concepts and Techniques of Productivity Measurement," *Monthly Labor Review* 102, no. 9 (September 1979), 23–27.

factor productivity). The following table of average annual rates of growth presents such an analysis for Japanese manufacturing between 1965 and 1973, when labor productivity grew at a remarkable 11.0 percent a year. Of this total, all but 0.8 percent a year resulted from an increase in capital, energy, and materials used per hour of labor input. Consequently, labor productivity grew quite rapidly while total-factor productivity, the measure of overall efficiency, grew rather slowly.

SOURCES OF JAPANESE PRODUCTIVITY GROWTH, 1965–1973	Percent Contribution
Capital-labor ratio	3.9
Energy-labor ratio	0.2
Materials-labor ratio	6.1
Total-factor productivity (overall efficiency)	0.8
Total growth in labor productivity	11.0

There are problems associated with total-factor productivity measurement. The most difficult is how to measure real capital input. However, these problems are less severe than they were several years ago, before the introduction of new measurement techniques and recent developments in the theory of production. A number of major U.S. firms now routinely measure total-factor productivity in ways that conform to the balance sheet and income statement of the firm. The American Telephone and Telegraph Company is an outstanding example.

SOURCE: J.R. Norsworthy, testimony on Recent Productivity Trends in the U.S. and Japan before the Subcommittee on Employment and Productivity, Senate Committee on Labor and Human Resources (97th Congress, 2nd session, 2 April 1982). For further information, see also U.S. Senate, Committee on Labor and Human Resources, *Productivity in the American Economy: Report and Findings* (Washington, D.C.: U.S. Government Printing Office, 1982).

HOW SERIOUS THE SLOWDOWN?

Virtually all observers agree that productivity growth in the United States began to decline during the last half of the 1960s. Most also agree that this decline occurred in two stages: the first extended from about 1965 through 1972; the second has continued at least through 1981. Labor productivity from the end of World War II to 1965 is usually estimated to have grown at an annual rate of about 3.2 percent or more. Then, during the 1965–1972 slowdown, it fell to between 2.0 and 2.5 percent a year. In the post-1972 period, it declined to an annual rate of less than one percent. For these same three periods, one set of estimates indicates that total-factor productivity grew consistently at a somewhat slower rate than labor productivity, declining from 2.6 percent in the initial postwar period, to 1.8 percent from 1966 to 1973, to less than 0.4 percent thereafter.

The slowdown has by no means been uniform (Figure 1). For example, productivity in communications has performed exceptionally well and agricultural productivity has also grown rapidly and consistently. Nevertheless, most of the economy has been heavily affected by this trend toward decline.

Indeed, the slowdown within the manufacturing sector has been widespread. The average annual percentage of growth in productivity after 1973 was lower than the average prior to 1973 in many major manufacturing industries (Figure 2).

The productivity slowdown is neither a recent nor a temporary phenomenon; it has been going on for more than fifteen years. Moreover, the decline is not negligible; productivity growth has fallen by about two-thirds from its early postwar level and this trend has been fairly widespread throughout the economy. Clearly, the slowdown is too substantial and too pervasive to be ignored.

U.S. AND FOREIGN PRODUCTIVITY PERFORMANCE

The picture that emerges when the U.S. record is compared with that of other leading industrial countries is at least as disturbing as the slowdown itself. But such a comparison may be mildly reassuring in two respects. First, the rather shaky figures comparing absolute productivity in the United States with that in other countries suggest that this country still occupies the leading position. Second, the United States is not alone in suffering a decline in productivity growth, and the drop it has experienced is comparable in magnitude to that in other industrialized countries. Four countries—

FIGURE 1

Changes in Total-Factor Productivity for Major Sectors, 1948–1981

Sector	Average Annual Rates of Change			
	1948–1965	1965–1973	1973–1979	1979–1981
Private domestic business	2.6	1.8	0.4	– 0.4
Manufacturing	2.6	2.3	0.8	– 0.4
Mining	2.3	1.7	– 4.0	– 1.3
Construction	2.4	– 1.0	– 3.0	– 2.5
Transportation	2.0	2.4	1.1	– 0.6
Communications	5.4	3.2	4.2	4.0
Public utilities	5.5	1.5	– 0.9	– 2.2
Trade (wholesale and retail)	2.4	2.6	0.6	– 0.7
Finance and insurance	1.0	0.3	– 1.0	– 1.6
Real estate	1.9	0.0	1.3	– 1.0
Services (professional and others)	0.3	– 0.1	0.1	1.0
Agriculture	3.6	1.3	1.8[a]	n.a.

a. Average annual rate of change for agriculture is for the 1973–1978 period.

n.a.: not available

SOURCE: American Productivity Center, *Productivity Perspectives*, rev. ed. (Houston: American Productivity Center, 1982).

FIGURE 2

Productivity-Growth Slowdown in Manufacturing Industries

Industry	Difference Between Average Annual Growth of Total-Factor Productivity Before and After 1973[a]
Food	−1.85
Tobacco	−1.19
Textiles	−0.67
Apparel	+1.79
Lumber	−2.63
Furniture	+2.16
Paper	−1.76
Printing	−2.26
Chemicals	−2.71
Petroleum	−4.86
Rubber	−1.53
Leather	+0.14
Stone, clay, glass	−0.48
Primary metals	−1.23
Fabricated metals	−0.50
Non-electrical machinery	−0.25
Electrical machinery	−0.83
Transportation equipment	−2.16
Instruments	−1.20
Miscellaneous manufacturing	−1.32

a. The difference before and after 1973 was obtained by comparing the 1953–1973 average annual growth with the 1973–1980 average annual growth.

SOURCE: Martin Neil Baily, "The Productivity Growth Slowdown by Industry," *Brookings Papers on Economic Activity*, no. 2 (1982). These are the preliminary results of a study that estimates total-factor productivity adjusted for utilization rates and cyclical variations.

Canada, Italy, Japan, and Sweden—experienced a reduction in productivity growth that was substantially greater than ours; three—the United Kingdom, France, and West Germany—suffered a significant deceleration as well (Figures 3 and 4).

However, that conclusion is just about the only comfort to be derived from these data. The statistics show that in virtually every case, both before and after the deeper phase of the slowdown began, U.S. productivity growth was below—and usually substantially below—growth in the other countries. In the earlier period, three of the countries experienced productivity growth nearly twice as rapid as ours, and two others achieved rates that were far more than twice as fast. Even in the second stage, the rate in four of the countries was more than double the U.S. rate.

Productivity is not the only area in which the American record has been unenviable; the rate of capital formation in the United States has been far from outstanding. For example, according to the economic forecasting firm Chase Econometrics, the amount of disposable personal income devoted to savings in 1980 was 21.0 percent in Japan, 15.5 percent in France, 15.0 percent in the United Kingdom, 13.2 percent in West Germany, and 10.3 percent in Canada, but it was only 5.6 percent in the United States.[2]

---

2. Edward Cowan, "Saving for a Sunnier Day: The Rationale," *New York Times*, 3 May 1981.

FIGURE 3

Average Annual Rates of Productivity Growth in Leading Industrialized Countries, 1960–1973 vs. 1973–1979 (Percent)

	1960–1973	1973–1979	Change
Italy	7.8	1.6	− 6.2
Japan	9.9	3.8	− 6.1
Sweden	5.8	2.5	− 3.3
Canada	4.2	1.0	− 3.2
United States	3.1	1.1	− 2.0
United Kingdom	3.8	1.9	− 1.9
France	5.9	4.2	− 1.7
West Germany	5.8	4.3	− 1.5

SOURCE: New York Stock Exchange, *U.S. Economic Performance in a Global Perspective* (New York: NYSE, 1981), 19.

That is, nearly every country cited saved at rates twice that of the United States. These differences in saving rates naturally tend to be reflected in rates of investment. The U.S. Bureau of Labor Statistics has indicated that for the period from 1970 to 1977, capital investment in manufacturing, calculated as a percentage of manufacturing output, was 26.5 percent in West Germany, 15.1 percent in Canada, and 9.6 percent in the United States.[3] Although the disparities among countries in manufacturing-investment rates are not quite as large as those in saving rates, they are still considerable, and every case in the small sample shows the United States in a markedly disadvantageous position. This is particularly disturbing because an unusually large proportion of U.S. investment in industry is devoted to replacing outmoded existing plant, which may make only a small contribution to productivity improvement, rather than to increasing its total capital stock.

Although these differences are significant as they stand, they will grow far more so if they persist for any substantial period of time. The phenomenon of compounding eventually transforms even small percentage differences into enormous disparities. Suppose, for example, that absolute productivity (however measured) in the United States were exactly the same as that in Japan but that Japan's were to grow at an average rate of 5 percent a year faster than ours. In fourteen years, the absolute level of productivity of an average Japanese worker would be about twice as large as that of the average U.S. worker; in twenty-eight years, his productivity level would exceed his counterpart's by a factor of four; and within forty-two years, it would be eight times as high. Both the saving and the investment rates given for the other countries average 8 to 9 percent higher than those for the United States. Thus, if their average total capital per unit of output were about the same as ours initially, it would double relative to that of the United States in about nine years, quadruple in eighteen years, and so on.

The figures that illustrate this "tyranny of compounding" are not meant to constitute a forecast. Certainly, there is every likelihood that such huge disparities will give rise to offsetting influences that will blunt the differences to some degree. The arithmetic projections are merely intended to show that the disparities among these growth rates, when taken by themselves, could have staggering long-run implications. Such figures suggest that unless some significant changes in relative growth rates occur, either fortuitously or through deliberate acts of policy, this country's economy

3. *Stimulating Technological Progress* (New York: CED, 1980), 23. The figures for West Germany are based on the 1970 to 1976 period.

FIGURE 4

Trends of Productivity Growth Rates: Indexed Labor Productivity-Growth Rates for Manufacturing Industries, 1960–1981

(For each country, 1960 equals 100)

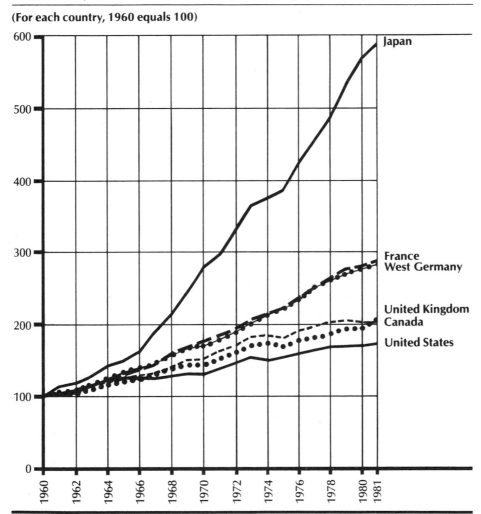

In order to compare productivity growth rates, each country's growth rate for 1960 is assigned a value of 100. If this figure were to compare *levels of productivity* (instead of growth rates), it would show each country starting at a different level. While the United States began at a higher level than did the other countries shown, by the end of the 1970s the more rapid growth rates in other countries resulted in a convergence of productivity levels in much of the manufacturing sector.

SOURCE: This figure was prepared from unpublished data provided by the U.S. Department of Labor, Bureau of Labor Statistics.

may well find itself reduced to third-rate status in terms of both its relative output and its relative standard of living. Such a decline would also have potentially disastrous social consequences.

It is essential to retain a sense of proportion about all this. Part of the success of the "miracle" economies of the Far East is attributable to the fact that their economies are at an earlier phase of industrialization. This has enabled them to benefit quickly from techniques and approaches accumulated over many years by the older industrial nations. As the Japanese and their neighbors begin to catch up with the industrialized countries of the West in absolute productivity levels, they will undoubtedly find it more difficult to maintain the differential between their growth rates and ours. At the same time, the pressures of the international marketplace will automatically spur U.S. industry to greater effort. Thus, there are many reasons to expect some automatic narrowing of the gap in productivity growth between the United States and the economies with which it competes.

Yet, this prospect does not justify complacency. Despite similar developments, countries that were economically preeminent in the past have toppled from their leading position; the Netherlands in the seventeenth and eighteenth centuries and the United Kingdom in the nineteenth and twentieth centuries learned this only too well. And it is obvious by now that imitation is by no means the only source of Japan's success. There is little reason for confidence that the United States can survive the challenge to its economic primacy without substantial outlays of thought, energy, and resources to productivity growth.

TOWARD POLICY: GENERAL CONSIDERATIONS

There is no shortage of policy prescriptions for stimulating productivity. The list of measures ranges from added stimuli for investment to improved training for workers to acceleration of deregulation. Later in this statement, we will examine these proposals in detail.

It must be understood that there is a difference between conditions that are *necessary* and conditions that are *sufficient* for solution of the problem. A policy that takes a necessary step toward solution of the productivity problem may be regarded as a commendable initial move without which there would be no hope of achieving the desired goal, but by itself is not adequate for that purpose. In contrast, a program that promises to be sufficient for the achievement of the selected goals is one that can be expected not only to move matters in the right direction but also to do so by the required magnitude. If, for example, we are trying to catch up with

Japan's 6 percent rate of productivity improvement in manufacturing, it is not sufficient to adopt policies capable of raising the U.S. manufacturing rate by only 2 percentage points, even if that accomplishes the necessary step of reversing the current trend. On the other hand, if we wish to remain competitive in manufacturing, we do not necessarily have to match the productivity-growth rates of our major competitors in all industries within the manufacturing sector, although we would have to achieve comparable productivity-growth records in most.

Discussions of productivity policy have tended to focus on necessary rather than sufficient conditions for achieving explicit or implicit goals. That focus has kept many discussions confined to fairly routine programs that would not cause very substantial changes in the way things are done. This has an attraction: anyone who sticks to the business-as-usual approach is not likely to be charged with impracticality. But mere tinkering with the status quo, although it may provide the necessary first step toward a solution of the productivity problem, will usually fall substantially short of the target and may even prove to be woefully insufficient.

The difference between necessary and sufficient measures is easy to illustrate. Many argue that reduction of taxes on business in general and business investment in particular, along with elimination of the more onerous government regulations, would do much to improve productivity, and there is a very good case to be made that such changes are a necessary part of an effective program to stimulate productivity growth. Even a casual comparison of government regulation in Taiwan and India, two countries with vastly disparate growth records (see "Regulation Makes a Difference: Taiwan and India," page 21), does confirm that overregulation can impose a debilitating handicap on an economy and its productivity performance. This comparison also suggests that efforts to reduce regulation in the United States are not misguided and that they may well be a necessary step in our productivity program.

But are reductions in taxation and regulation sufficient for that purpose? The case of the United Kingdom during the half century it took for its economy to lose its preeminence suggests the contrary. Most observers agree that British economic growth began its absolute and relative decline between 1870 and 1914. According to one study, its rate of growth of industrial output per man-year fell fairly steadily from 1.2 percent between 1870 and 1880 to 0.2 percent between 1890 and 1913.[4] Another estimate indicates that over the same period, output per man-hour grew 1.5 percent

---

4. Derek H. Aldcroft and Harry W. Richardson, *The British Economy 1870–1939* (London: Macmillan & Co., 1969), 126.

a year in the United Kingdom, 1.8 percent in France, 2.1 percent in Germany, and 2.3 percent in the United States.[5] Yet—except for some legislation designed to protect gasworks against the incursions of electricity and railroads from the competition of automobiles—the British economy was essentially one in which the free market and free trade prevailed. There is probably no example of a major country with a less regulated economy in recent history. Alone, deregulation and reduced taxation will not guarantee success.

An essential distinction is between the short-term and the long-term possibilities for productivity improvement. Over the next few years, productivity increases must be derived almost entirely from better use of the resources now in place: existing plant, equipment, work force, management, and techniques. Only in the long run can productivity be improved by replacement of obsolete plant and equipment, better education of the work force, more effective managerial performance, and the introduction of new techniques.

Stimulus to the nation's productivity growth can originate from major innovations in products, processes, or both. It can also be obtained by gradual improvements in the use of currently available resources, for example, by providing employees with incentives to improve their work effort.

The most dramatic improvements in productivity arise from major innovations in the physical product, or in the production process, or in service itself, rather than from gradual improvements in day-to-day efficiency. In the short run, however, dramatic innovation in individual establishments will have little measurable effect on the productivity of the economy as a whole. Dramatic innovation, whether it involves new products or radical new processes, will improve the nation's overall productivity performance only after a considerable period of time, after it is diffused throughout the economy, and has perhaps led to a stream of related innovations. Moreover, some significant product innovations can yield their benefits in ways that cannot be measured precisely, if at all.

Many of the required changes will begin to show up in the overall statistics only after a number of years have passed. It would be a great mistake to confuse short-term issues with long-term issues and to expect short-term improvements from actions of basic importance that are taken now but will make themselves felt only gradually in the years ahead. For example, new depreciation rates will affect corporate cash flows and profits, and the individual retirement account (IRA) legislation may in-

---

5. Trevor May, *The Economy 1815–1914* (London: Collins, 1972), 163.

REGULATION MAKES A DIFFERENCE:
TAIWAN AND INDIA

Both Taiwan and India started from similarly low levels of per capita GNP in the late 1950s; in 1958, Taiwan's gross domestic product per capita was $98, and India's was $69. By 1979, India's GNP per capita was only $190, whereas the figure for Taiwan was $1,868. Taiwan's growth in GDP per capita averaged about 7 percent a year between 1951 and 1976; India's average was about 1.1 percent. Between 1950 and 1971, India's average annual increase in national income was the lowest in the world.

Many factors influence this enormous difference in performance, but evidence indicates that a substantial role was played by government regulation. Beginning in the 1950s, the government of Taiwan adopted a policy of liberalization of industrial production and trade and gradual abolition of exchange controls. A five-year exemption from corporate taxes was granted for new investments, and the maximum corporate tax was set at 25 percent. By the 1970s, exports were manufactured under virtually free-trade conditions. Initial restrictions on the establishment of new businesses were gradually removed. The Indian economy, in contrast, is a jungle of regulation. For example, any firm whose total investment in land, buildings, plant, and machinery exceeds 10 million rupees (approximately $1 million) is required to have a license to operate; and that license specifies, among other things, size of output, location, production methods, raw materials, and fuels. Over 500 lines of production are reserved for small-scale businesses and prohibited to medium- and large-scale enterprises (defined as firms whose capital exceeds one million rupees, or $100,000). The list includes domestic electric appliances, laundry soap, bicycle tires and tubes, and a variety of automobile parts.

SOURCES: *United Nations Yearbook of National Accounts Statistics*, International Tables, 1971 and 1979 (New York: United Nations, 1971 and 1980), 5, and 3 and 185.

Council for Economic Planning and Development, *Taiwan Statistical Date Book 1980* (Republic of China: Government of the Republic of China, June 1980), 25.

Simon Kuznets, "Growth and Structural Shifts" in *Economic Growth and Structural Change in Taiwan*, ed. Walter Galenson (Ithaca, N.Y.: Cornell University Press, 1979), 127.

Lawrence J. White, "Technology and Development: Some Indirect Evidence" (New York: New York University, 1980, photocopy).

P. K. Ghosh, *Government and Industry: Studies in Regulatory Policy and Practices* (Calcutta: Allahabad, 1977).

fluence individual savings. But the effects of these changes will show up slowly in the overall level of capital investment and even more slowly in the resulting increase in productivity. To expect short-term results from long-term measures is to risk disillusionment and abandonment of constructive changes before they have had the chance to work.

CAUSES AND REMEDIES

It is often claimed that information about the causes of a problem is tantamount to knowledge of its solution. Such a view assumes that the appropriate remedies are the reverse of the causes. Sometimes such an inference is valid; for example, inflationary pressures generated by a growing federal deficit can be reduced by a decrease in public expenditures. But things do not always work that way. Economic recovery from a recession may require a reduction in interest rates even though in that case interest rates bear no responsibility for the recession.

Indeed, it is probably fortunate that the solution to a problem is not always a mere reversal of its causes. Sometimes causes may turn out to be highly intractable and largely beyond the reach of public policy, and, in fact, we will see that this is true of some of the major influences to which the productivity slowdown has been ascribed. The possibility that policies unrelated to such causes can nevertheless be effective may then prove welcome. For example, some statistical analysts have concluded that a significant source of the productivity problem is the continuing shift of the U.S. labor force away from manufacturing and agriculture to the services. The evidence confirms that, on the average, productivity increases in many of the services (with some noteworthy exceptions, such as communications) are harder to achieve and occur much more slowly than those in manufacturing. However, it is doubtful whether public policy can (or should) do anything to alter the trends in consumer tastes that are the source of such employment patterns.

CHAPTER 3

WHY WORRY ABOUT PRODUCTIVITY?

Is all the concern about productivity really justified? Is productivity all that important for the public welfare? The answers to these questions are not quite as obvious as they may seem. Productivity does indeed affect the country in a number of very important ways, but some of the alleged consequences of increased or lagging productivity do not stand up to close examination.

Productivity has a direct influence on a nation's standard of living. As long as the ratio of the employed labor force to overall population does not change, and as long as hours of labor per worker remain constant, it follows mathematically that movements in per capita income must precisely follow those in average output per worker. If output per worker increases, per capita income must go up commensurately and members of the working community will benefit from increased productivity growth. Conversely, any economy whose labor-productivity growth lags persistently behind that of others must eventually experience a relatively (although not absolutely) lower standard of living. An example of this is the United Kingdom, whose per capita income is now only slightly more than half that in Sweden, West Germany, the Netherlands, France, and a number of other European countries.

This does not mean that the income of everyone in an economy can be expected to keep pace with productivity; the market mechanism does not normally distribute gains equally. In fact, it stimulates productivity growth by offering a larger share of the expanding output to those who have contributed most successfully to that expansion.

Growth in productivity can also provide support to programs designed to combat poverty and improve social conditions. A stagnant economy is likely to produce social and political stress among groups within society. Experience confirms that only in periods when rising productivity permits widespread increases in real income is the public willing to provide the resources necessary for improving the nation's well-being.

The same is true more generally of the nation's aspirations for a cleaner environment and an enhanced quality of life. There is strong evidence that these goals continue to occupy a high place on the public's list of priorities, but pursuit of these objectives is costly. For example, a reduction in the emissions levels of production processes usually requires additional resources. Waste-treatment plants, automobile emission controls, and smokestack scrubbers all have substantial real costs, and only an economy whose productivity is growing rapidly will be able to marshal the required resources without unacceptable sacrifice. Productivity growth can also help the nation to provide for its elderly. This problem is likely to become critical as the ratio of the number of dependent elderly to the working population increases because of the end of the baby boom and the rise in longevity. Without growing productivity it will be impossible to prevent a decline in the living standards of the elderly without cutting into the real incomes of the working-age population.

It is essential to make a convincing argument for increased productivity because of the social dislocations that are likely to accompany growth. Productivity growth can require movement of people from one occupation or geographic location to another, or of resources from one industry to another, and the social costs cannot be ignored. The huge gains in U.S. agricultural productivity, for example, were facilitated by the availability of industries and social programs capable of absorbing the former agricultural workers and of facilitating their transfer.

There are some who argue that the nation will have to reconcile itself to reduced economic growth because growth consumes natural resources, creates wastes, and causes environmental damage. But those who hold this view do not seem to realize that growth provides the means necessary for the realization of their objectives. Moreover, if we ensure that growth is achieved through enhanced productivity in the *use* of its inputs, rather than through increased quantities of inputs, we will be able to have things both ways—to enjoy increased outputs without commensurate increases in the use of resources or in the creation of wastes.

Growth in productivity also can benefit some of the industries most heavily affected by foreign competition. The relatively poor productivity performance of U.S. industry in recent years has handicapped a number of American industries not only in their efforts to hold their own in foreign markets but also in their attempts to retain their share of the domestic market. A few years ago, foreign manufacturers could hope for no better than negligible positions in the American market for mass-produced items; today, however, U.S. producers of automobiles, electronic equipment, bicycles, motorcycles, small appliances, cameras, and many other goods find that foreign producers have captured large shares of U.S. sales volume. As real wages in a dozen countries approach and perhaps exceed our own, the success of foreign producers in the fields in which we have fallen behind can no longer be ascribed to the availability of cheap foreign labor. Rather, the explanation lies to a considerable degree in the improved quality of the successful foreign products and the rise in productivity in those industries. In the short run, other factors such as the recent appreciation of the U.S. dollar can affect relative prices among countries. This explanation has not been a major factor in the long-run loss of competitiveness of some U.S. products.

If the growth of U.S. productivity continues to lag behind that of other industrialized countries for any substantial period of time, the nation will pay a heavy price. It is true that even in such circumstances, this country will nevertheless move in the direction of restoring the balance-of-payments equilibrium in the long run and new export industries must arise to replace those that cannot compete. However, *persistently poor productivity performance will eventually force any nation to compete in international markets, not on the basis of strength, but through unfair trade practices or relatively low real wages and profits, which offset the effects of a relatively low productivity level on costs.* This trend is sure to elicit increased demands for protection from foreign competition by industries that fall behind in comparative efficiency, and these may well reduce the economy's flexibility and responsiveness to opportunities for technological change.

Many are convinced that productivity growth can be a potent weapon in the war against inflation. On the other hand, increased productivity has been viewed with some alarm as a cause of unemployment. In both cases, however, matters are not quite what they seem at first.

There is no question that productivity growth and inflation are related. If input costs increase no more rapidly than total-factor productivity improves, prices can remain steady. For example, if input prices increase 5 percent in a year but each unit of input yields, on the average, 5 percent more product, output prices need not rise at all. But when increases in wages and in prices of other inputs outrun the growth in productivity, the cost per unit of output rises. Thus, the relationship between productivity growth and inflation is close and direct. All other things being equal, the more rapid the rate of productivity growth, the lower the rate of inflation.

Unfortunately, stimulation of productivity growth is not by itself a promising weapon with which to combat inflation in the short run. A successful program to encourage productivity will certainly move matters in the right direction, but its effects on inflation will take years to reach significant proportions. Other programs, in addition, will undoubtedly be required for the battle against inflation. For example, even if by some miracle, a trebling of the present growth rate in total-factor productivity could be achieved overnight, raising it from less than one percent to as much as 3 percent, such growth would reduce the inflation rate only by 3 percentage points, and even that would be possible only if the rate of wage increase did not rise as a result. To decrease the inflation rate by 6 percentage points through a productivity-stimulation program alone, productivity growth also would have to be increased by 6 percentage points, something that does not seem even remotely within reach in just a few years.

Productivity improvements may affect the collective bargaining process and the wage-price relationship in ways that help to contain inflation.[1] Also, success on the productivity front may simply change the general economic atmosphere and the character of expectations in a way that contributes to the long-run anti-inflation goal. Nevertheless, *it must be emphasized that productivity policy is important primarily because of its long-run relevance for living standards, including the quality of life, not for its short-run effect on inflation.*

---

1. See William C. Freund and Paul D. Manchester, "Productivity and Inflation" (Houston: American Productivity Center, 1980, photocopy). Of course, increasing productivity may affect wage bargaining the other way, stimulating greater demands and thereby exacerbating inflation.

If productivity growth promises less than some had hoped on the inflation front, it also threatens less than some had feared in the field of employment. Indeed, in the long run, there is virtually no connection between productivity growth and loss of jobs. In the short run, employees who resist innovations that would increase productivity growth may even have been right to some degree in terms of their immediate self-interest. Except where institutional arrangements such as those in Japan and the Israeli kibbutzim offer some assurance that workers will not be displaced, employers may well be tempted to remove from their labor force those workers whom new machines have replaced.

In the long run, matters are quite different. The output of any economy generally does not stay still; it usually expands. The workyear per employee does not remain constant either; it declines as the standard of living improves. For both reasons, over longer periods, even though productivity has grown spectacularly, involuntary unemployment has shown no tendency to rise. It is estimated that since 1800, the productivity of labor in the United States has grown at least twentyfold, thanks to the continuing and cumulative flow of technological improvement and other influences. Even given this dramatic increase in productivity, the rate of involuntary unemployment has hardly changed from 1800 to the present.

Thus, neither history nor logic provides any foundation for fears that growing productivity will saddle the economy with intractable unemployment. If fiscal and monetary policies cannot cope with the problem, market forces will, as growing national output absorbs the workers released by expanded productivity.

PRODUCTIVITY AND INTERNATIONAL COMPETITIVE POSITION

In the international marketplace, U.S. industry is already beginning to feel the effects of lagging productivity growth. In the 1960s and 1970s, a number of American industries found it difficult to retain their shares of foreign markets. Moreover, they witnessed the successful invasion of U.S. markets by foreign products. Imports of automobiles, television sets, radio equipment, and cameras are only some of the most obvious examples.

It has been charged that export subsidies by foreign governments helped start this invasion and that U.S. industry's export problems are partly due to various types of restrictions and impediments that other countries have imposed on American imports. Although the strength of the U.S. dollar has reduced the competitiveness of U.S. goods abroad, it seems clear that neither a stronger dollar nor domestic subsidies by foreign governments are the entire problem. U.S. industry has found itself increasingly handicapped in the competitive race by its lagging productivity performance and the rising relative costs that accompany that lag.

It is tempting to conclude that unless this country's productivity growth succeeds in maintaining a level at or above its competitors', some U.S. industries are fated to be driven out of foreign markets and to have much of their home market taken over by foreign producers. This conjures up a vision of a growing and chronic balance-of-payments disequilibrium, with the United States finding it increasingly difficult to earn the foreign exchange necessary to pay for essential imports. But although lagging productivity growth will, indeed, exact a heavy cost in terms of relative economic position, it will certainly not, in the long run, take the form of either an inability to sell U.S. goods abroad or a rising balance-of-payments deficit.

Even if the United States were to end up being less proficient than other countries in the production of every one of its outputs, other countries would continue to import at least some products from us. A country whose poor productivity renders it a less efficient producer of all its goods will not be driven completely from the international marketplace. As the well-established principle of *comparative advantage* has demonstrated, it will benefit efficient nations, when their capacity is fully utilized, to purchase from the productivity laggard those goods in whose supply it is *less inefficient*. Such a situation enables efficient countries to specialize, devoting their resources largely to the production of those items they produce best. True, the inefficient country may find itself left with the crumbs, confined to the production of items that are, in effect, disdained by its rivals, but it can be confident that it will retain a niche in the market, although its standard of living will decline.

In practice, matters are usually complicated by government interference with freedom of trade and the workings of market forces. For example, differences in monetary policy from country to country can sometimes disrupt the process by which equilibrium in exchange rates is maintained. Before such equilibrium is reached, domestic and international political pressures can negate the process by increased protectionism. This, in turn, compounds the problem of improving productivity. We do not operate in an international marketplace in which trade is completely free and in which governments refrain from measures that impede imports or offer "unfair" subsidies to exports. Nations that are victimized by such acts may feel forced to adopt countermeasures. That, of course, is not the subject of this report, but it is an issue that merits examination elsewhere.

Although balance-of-payments disequilibrium is eventually self-correcting, the cure is certainly painful. It involves decreasing relative incomes in the deficit countries, aggravated by changes in prices and exchange rates for the deficit and surplus countries. Each of these changes means that the deficit country tends, at least in the short run, to sell its export products at lower prices and buy its imports at higher prices. Thus, the deficit country must reconcile itself to receiving smaller and smaller quantities of goods and services in exchange for its labor in comparison with other countries until the relative price of its labor becomes low enough to restore its international competitiveness.

These conclusions are not meant to be comforting. In such circumstances, the promised equilibrium of exports and imports is indeed restored, but the cost is one that most Americans would consider unacceptable: a drastic reduction in the American standard of living relative to that prevailing in the rest of the world.

CHAPTER 4

ON THE CAUSES OF THE PRODUCTIVITY SLOWDOWN

There are many statistical studies of the productivity slowdown and its causes.[1] They generally agree on the magnitude of the slowdown, and seem to agree on possible causes, many of which can be tested statistically. The statistics have been used to measure what happens when there is a change in the behavior of:

- investment in research and development, which provides the basis for innovation and technological progress;

- the rate of capital formation in the form of plant and equipment (as affected by the level of saving and investment);

- the composition of output (that is, the distribution of GNP between goods and services whose productivity typically grows rapidly and those whose productivity growth is relatively slow);

---

1. Edward N. Wolff, "The Magnitude and Causes of the Recent Productivity Slowdown in the U.S.: A Survey of Recent Studies" in *Stimulation of U.S. Productivity Growth,* ed. William J. Baumol and Kenneth McLennan (forthcoming). Much of this chapter is based on this survey, which was prepared as a background paper for CED. A partial list of the studies assessed appears in Figure 7.

- the composition of the labor force in terms of age, race, sex, education, and work experience;
- the availability and cost of natural resources, especially those related to energy;
- government activities, particularly in the form of regulation.

In addition to the possible causes that can be evaluated by statistical evidence, a number of hypotheses about causes of the slowdown are based on general observation and judgment. Some influences that have been suggested include:

- excessive preoccupation of business management with the short-term rather than the long-term consequences of its decisions;
- a general decline in the spirit of entrepreneurship through management-reward systems that encourage avoidance of risk rather than innovation;
- inflation, which has created uncertainty, absorbing the time and effort of management, and increasing the real cost of resources for investment;
- a deterioration in the quality of investment decisions, partly attributable to investments in inflation hedges rather than in additions to the nation's productive capacity;
- growth in domestic protectionism, involving the rescue of firms threatened by bankruptcy and the imposition of antitrust and regulatory measures against vigorous competition, all of which reduce the pressures on management to devote resources and energy to innovation and productivity growth;
- defense outlays that consume resources that could otherwise have been used in higher-productivity activities;
- financing difficulties for small firms;
- the role of the unions, including resistance to technological change and support of featherbedding (contentions that have, of course, been disputed hotly).

This list does not pretend to be complete. It merely illustrates the great variety of causes of the productivity slowdown that have been proposed. There is little agreement among either casual observers or experts about the share of responsibility that must be borne by any one influence, and the fact that the growth of productivity and the influences that determine it vary enormously from industry to industry has contributed to this lack of consensus.

Even those who have used formal statistical techniques to quantify the comparative importance of the possible causes of the productivity deceleration have obtained results that disagree substantially with one another. The figures cited in this chapter illustrate that there is probably no single cause that can explain more than half of the slowdown. Despite substantial disagreement on their *relative* significance, there is a consensus among researchers that the following are the most important reasons for the U.S. decline in productivity growth. Indeed, since so many factors can contribute to a slowdown in productivity growth, any single factor that accounts for more than 10 or 15 percent of the slowdown is of major significance. Policies affecting such factors should be high on the nation's agenda for improving U.S. productivity.

CAPITAL FORMATION

Although it is true that saving and investment rates in the United States are lower than those in other industrialized countries, the magnitude of the effect of this variable on the productivity slowdown is not easy to judge. Gross private domestic investment actually rose about 10 percent relative to gross domestic production during the first period of the productivity slowdown (about 1965 to 1973). This ratio declined somewhat thereafter but has remained well above its early postwar level. More important, however, the capital-to-labor ratio actually declined because of the simultaneous increase in the labor force during the same period. Because there are differences among the ways investigators calculate investment figures, the magnitude of that decline is by no means agreed upon.[2] Most studies attribute between 20 and 40 percent of the productivity decline to the behavior of investment. Other estimates ascribe some 50 percent or more of the slowdown to this source (Figure 5). The evidence suggests that the role of capital formation—that is, the increase in new plant and equipment— was relatively unimportant before 1973 but probably did become significant during the second phase.

---

2. Among the relevant issues is whether private homes and the capital of nonprofit organizations should be included in the figure for the nation's capital stock. Perhaps equally important in this respect is the amount of new capital devoted to pollution control and compliance.

FIGURE 5

Contribution of Capital Formation

Estimated Percent of Responsibility for Slowdown

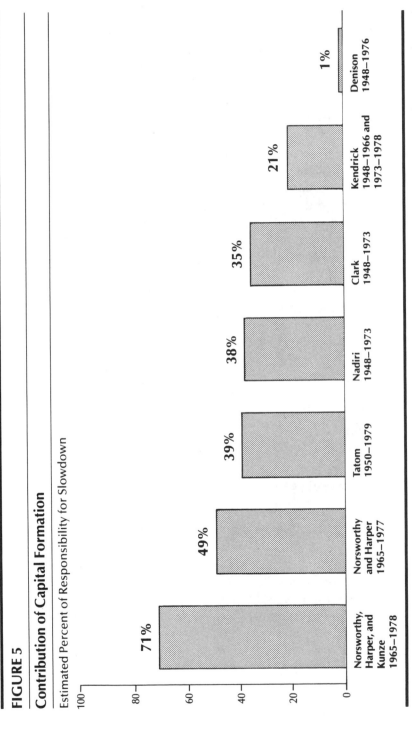

SOURCE: Edward N. Wolff, "The Magnitude and Causes of the Recent Productivity Slowdown in the U.S.: A Survey of Recent Studies" in *Stimulation of U.S. Productivity Growth*, ed. William J. Baumol and Kenneth McLennan (forthcoming). Complete bibliographical information about the studies cited above appears in Figure 7.

A review of the research suggests that insufficient capital formation was a more important explanation for the decline in productivity-growth rates in nonmanufacturing industries than for the decline that occurred in most manufacturing industries after 1973. Because of differences in capital intensiveness and depreciation of capital stock among industries, the significance of lack of capital formation undoubtedly varies from industry to industry. For example, even after adjusting for the effects of regulation on productivity growth, during the 1970s the capital-to-labor ratio declined in such industries as autos and steel, implying that lack of capital formation is an important cause of the decline in productivity in these industries.

While insufficient capital formation may only partially explain the U.S. slowdown in productivity growth since 1973, our lower rate of investment in plant and equipment compared to the investment rates in other countries is an even more important reason that our productivity-growth rates have been consistently lower than the productivity performance of other major industrial nations (see Chapter 5).

Investment can also retard or stimulate productivity indirectly. New capital equipment is generally of the most modern design. Thus, an increase in the rate of investment means that an economy's plant and equipment will incorporate most recent technological changes, whereas a decline in investment means that capital stock will become increasingly obsolete. Several analysts have concluded that there has, in fact, been such an effect, with the average age of plant and equipment declining quite substantially between 1948 and 1966 and then leveling off. On the other hand, one investigator has attributed less than one tenth of the decline in productivity growth after 1973 to this source.[3]

RESEARCH AND DEVELOPMENT OUTLAYS

Research and development expenditures do not seem to have played the most critical role in the slowdown (Figure 6). Although the ratio of research and development expenditures to GNP fell from 2.97 percent in 1964 to 2.27 percent in the 1976–1977 interval, the decline primarily represents cuts in the military and space programs. Outlays for nonmilitary research have fluctuated, but they have actually risen in absolute terms and even in relation to GNP (by more than 10 percent) over the period as a whole. Consequently, it is not surprising that almost all investigators who

3. Peter K. Clark, "Issues in the Analysis of Capital Formation and Productivity Growth," *Brookings Papers on Economic Activity*, no. 2 (Washington, D.C.: Brookings Institution, 1979), 423–431.

eliminate military and space research and development from their expenditure figures conclude that little (if any) of the productivity slowdown can be traced to this variable.

Nevertheless, there are some disturbing facts even in this area. One recent study reports that private industry in the United States employed 5 percent *fewer* scientists and engineers in 1975 than in 1970. Also, the share of U.S. patents granted to foreign inventors rose from 20 percent in 1966 to 38 percent in 1978, indicating that other industrial nations are now increasing their output of successful R&D.[4]

4. U.S. Department of Commerce, Patent and Trade Office, Office of Technology Assessment and Forecasts, "OTAF Special Report—All Technologies Report, January 1963 to June 1982" (Arlington, Va.: 1982, photocopy).

FIGURE 6

Contribution of Insufficient R&D

Estimated Percent of Responsibility for Slowdown

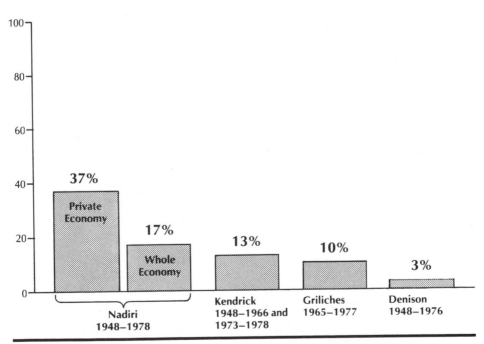

SOURCE: Wolff, "Magnitude and Causes of the Recent Productivity Slowdown." Complete bibliographical information about the studies cited above appears in Figure 7.

COMPOSITION OF OUTPUT

The shift in the composition of the labor force from manufacturing and agricultural workers to service employees is a particularly controversial variable. It is generally agreed that productivity growth in many (but by no means all) services, and especially in personal services, is far slower than it is in manufacturing and agriculture, and the record confirms this. Therefore, if a constant share of real GNP is contributed by those services whose productivity growth is slow, their share of the labor force will rise because the output per worker in manufacturing will rise relative to per-worker output in those services. For example, suppose that productivity grows at a rate of 3 percent a year in manufacturing but only one percent a year in the services, and that the outputs of both sectors expand by exactly 2 percent a year. At the end of a year, the services will have to employ more workers than they did in the beginning, but manufacturing will need a smaller labor force.

Something like this has apparently happened. For example, the share of real service output may not have increased very much during the postwar period, but between 1948 and 1969, the share of total employment in service industries rose from 54 to 64 percent. A greater shift occurred in agriculture, with unskilled labor moving to other sectors of the economy as a result of increased agricultural productivity.

Some who have investigated the contribution of changes in the value of output produced by different sectors have concluded that such changes have not accounted for any significant part of the productivity slowdown. On the other hand, studies of the effect of the *allocation of the labor force* among sectors have arrived at a different conclusion, in some cases attributing as much as half of the problem to this source.

The research that shows virtually no effect of changing composition of output on the productivity slowdown was based on the shift from the farming to the nonfarming sector. This is too broad an industry breakdown to determine the significance of output changes in a diversified economy. Similarly, the studies that attribute virtually all of the slowdown to changing composition were conducted using data up to about 1970 and cannot explain the slowdown that occurred after 1973. Among the remaining studies, which use later data, there is considerable disagreement over the appropriate means of measuring the effect of output changes. Nevertheless, there is general agreement that even if composition of output had some role in explaining the productivity slowdown that occurred in the 1960s, such changes were less important in the 1973 slowdown.[5]

---

5. Wolff, "The Magnitude and Causes of the Recent Productivity Slowdown in the U.S."

COMPOSITION OF THE LABOR FORCE

The changing role in the labor force of minority groups, women, and young workers, and the trend toward a better-educated labor force are generally believed to have had substantial effects on productivity growth. However, some of these effects may have offset others, so that, on balance, the composition of the labor force may have made relatively little net difference.

Both the rise in the proportion of younger and less experienced workers that occurred as a result of the baby boom and the increased participation of women in the labor force seem to have slowed productivity growth somewhat, at least in the earlier period. The seriousness of this problem will decline since the proportion of young women in higher education is now equal to that of young men. Moreover, during the next two decades the average educational level of the U.S. labor force will be higher than at any time in our history.

The education and training of the work force have been improving, and observers agree that over time this has stimulated productivity growth. Yet, a significant proportion of youths are receiving a relatively poor education, and there is considerable concern that current approaches to the education and training of the labor force are leaving a group of hard-to-employ people unprepared for the job requirements of the decades ahead.

ENERGY PRICES AND NATURAL RESOURCES

The sharp rise in energy prices has contributed to inflation and to a reduction in the nation's net output. Higher energy costs, by reducing demand, affected the production of goods generally and also led to investment designed to permit the substitution of other inputs of energy, all of which reduced the net output of the economy. Most statistical studies have shown that although the energy problem influenced the productivity slowdown, its direct contribution was probably small (Figure 7). This is because the share of energy as an input is small compared with those of other inputs for U.S. industry as a whole.

It seems clear, however, that energy problems in the United States have been a far more significant impediment to productivity growth than the numerical data show. The behavior of world productivity growth immediately after each of the major fuel crises of the 1970's leaves little doubt on the subject. The sharp rise of energy prices after 1973 had an important *indirect* effect on the productivity slowdown. Energy and capital are used in conjunction with each other, and when the capital input increases, so does the associated energy input. The 1973 energy-price increase discouraged U.S. business from using both energy and capital. In time, new plant and equipment can be made energy efficient, but a rapid rise in energy prices indirectly contributes to the productivity slowdown by reducing the growth of the capital-to-labor ratio. The growth of the capital-to-labor ratio is further retarded because rising energy prices encourage business to substitute labor for capital.

GOVERNMENT REGULATION

No one denies that regulations relating to environmental, health, safety, and similar concerns have consumed a portion of GNP—perhaps about 3 percent in some years—that would otherwise have gone into ordinary goods and services. The diversion of resources has produced a less efficient allocation of capital and labor, thus reducing the productive potential of the economy. In general, studies agree that such regulations have contributed perhaps 10 to 15 percent of the productivity slowdown in several ways: by reducing the speed and effectiveness with which business decision makers can respond to changing market conditions; by reallocating resources toward less productive activities; and by increasing the uncertainty of business about future regulation. And unintentionally, regulations have favored old plant and equipment over new through the imposition of higher regulatory standards upon these new plants. Excessive regulations have also raised the cost of new plant and equipment. This has discouraged the replacement and modernization of the nation's capital stock.

Statistical analyses also seem to agree that the measurable effects of regulation on productivity growth have been important, but not enormous. But here again, there may be significant unquantifiable effects stemming from diversion of resources, inhibition of the ability or willingness of business to take advantage of promising opportunities, and sheer paper work and red tape, all of which may be quite substantial.

It is also important to remember that regulations that protect the environment or the safety of workers certainly yield benefits and add to our real standard of living in ways that the GNP does not take into account. These difficult-to-measure benefits from regulation will partially offset apparent reduced productivity growth resulting from the increase in government regulation.

FIGURE 7

Contribution of Energy Prices

Estimated Percent of Responsibility for Slowdown

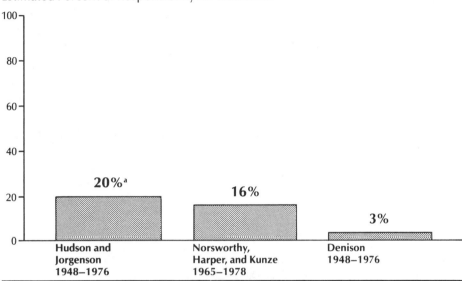

a. This percentage-contribution figure is an approximation, based on Denison's estimate of a 2.97 percentage-point decline in overall productivity growth.

SOURCE: Wolff, "Magnitude and Causes of the Recent Productivity Slowdown."

The data in Figures 5, 6, and 7 originally appeared in the following studies:

Peter K. Clark, "Issues in the Analysis of Capital Formation and Productivity Growth," *Brookings Papers on Economic Activity,* no. 2 (1979), 423–431.

Edward F. Denison, *Accounting for Slower Economic Growth* (Washington, D.C.: Brookings Institution, 1979).

Zvi Griliches, "R&D and the Productivity Slowdown," *American Economic Review* 70, no. 2 (May 1980), 343–347.

E. A. Hudson and Dale W. Jorgenson, "Energy Prices and the U.S. Economy, 1972–1976," *National Resources Journal* 18, no. 4 (October 1978), 877–897.

John Kendrick, "Productivity Trends in the United States," in *Lagging Productivity Growth,* ed. Shlomo Maital and Noah M. Meltz (Cambridge, Mass.: Ballinger, 1980).

M. Ishaq Nadiri, "Sectoral Productivity Slowdown," *American Economic Review* 70, no. 2 (May 1980), 349–352.

J. R. Norsworthy and Michael J. Harper, "The Role of Capital Formation in the Recent Slowdown in Productivity Growth," Bureau of Labor Statistics Working Paper No. 87 (January 1979).

J. R. Norsworthy, Michael J. Harper, and K. Kunze, "The Slowdown in Productivity Growth: Analysis of Some Contributing Factors," *Brookings Papers on Economic Activity,* no. 2 (1979), 387–421.

John A. Tatom, "The Productivity Problem," *Federal Reserve Bank of St. Louis Monthly Review* (September 1979), 3–16.

BUSINESS FLUCTUATIONS

There is a clear and well-documented relationship between productivity and the stages of the business cycle. During a downturn, companies do not lay off workers at a rate proportional to the business decline. Consequently, labor productivity (the ratio of output to labor input) tends to decline during the downturn. In the initial upturn the reverse is the case and productivity rises.

To the extent that the productivity decline after 1973 can be attributed to cyclical influences, the problem may be transitory. However, the bulk of the evidence seems to show that this influence has been minor. In any event, the fact that more than eighteen years have elapsed since the productivity slowdown began suggests that much more than a cyclical phenomenon is involved. Perhaps a long period of sluggish economic activity also hurts productivity growth, but there seems to be no hard evidence to bear this out.

EVALUATING THE STATISTICAL INDICATORS

Obviously, the statistical evidence on the sources of the productivity slowdown is insufficient to rank the major causes in order of importance. Research, however, does suggest that an insufficient rate of capital formation probably played a leading role. Regulation has also probably played an important part, and rising energy prices also appear to have had more influence than statistical measurement shows. The share of the labor force employed in the services may have made a contribution, although this conclusion is particularly controversial. Research has also shown that the relative importance of these major sources varies by type of industry and service, but that the nature of these variations is somewhat uncertain. All in all, while research has identified the major contributors to the overall problem, the state of information on the subject is far from satisfactory.

OTHER IMPEDIMENTS TO PRODUCTIVITY GROWTH

The limitations of available data leave any list of possible causes of the slowdown incomplete, and the complexity of the statistical problems—and of the economic system itself—makes the conclusions equivocal. Non-statistical observation offers presumptions well beyond the conclusions of statistical analyses. For example, military spending, which makes up a much larger share of GNP in the United States than it does in Japan, is cited by some as a possible influence on declining productivity improvement. An increase in defense outlays serves to drain off resources that otherwise might have gone into investment or consumption. The defense sector employs a significant proportion of the nation's scientific and technical personnel whose training, experience, and technological innovations have important applications in the private sector. It has been suggested, however, that as military equipment has grown increasingly specialized, the rate of transfer of technology from the military to the civilian sector has declined.

Another potential cause of the productivity decline is the tendency toward domestic protectionism that benefits particular industries or firms but weakens the economy as a whole. Government aid to those threatened by bankruptcy is perhaps the most publicized manifestation of this phenomenon. Antitrust and regulatory policies may also make a contribution; regulators, for example, have a long history of protecting firms from new competitors. Antitrust agencies have tended to single out successful enterprises for highly publicized action, thereby protecting enterprises unable to win in the marketplace through their own efficiency and ingenuity. Businesses themselves frequently resort to the courts to obtain protection from their successful rivals. Such protectionism can sap the vitality of the market mechanism, reward inefficiency, and inhibit prompt action by the managements of efficient firms. The litigiousness in our society may also inhibit managerial decisiveness by making business unwilling to take action if there is any risk of litigation. A plausible case can consequently be made for the view that this tendency contributes significantly to reduced risk taking and quality in managerial performance.

One significant omission from the earlier list of causes of declining productivity growth is inflation. If nothing else, inflation has been an enormous drain on human resources, distracting management and individuals from the activities that help to generate real economic benefits. Companies and individuals have devoted inordinate amounts of time and effort to the search for means of preventing the value of their financial assets from erosion and of coping with the threat of an increased tax burden that would result from tax rates that were not indexed for inflation. During an inflationary period, additional investment funds must be raised to keep abreast of the price level. Inflation makes long-term borrowing extremely risky because the high nominal interest rates that accompany rising prices may well prove to be highly disadvantageous when the inflation decelerates and interest rates on new borrowings fall correspondingly. Inflation can also have drastic consequences for lending institutions that have made long-term commitments to borrowers.

Inflation has upset the capital markets, depressing the real value of stocks, making it far more expensive for firms to acquire new equity capital, and increasing their vulnerability to disturbing influences such as takeover attempts. In addition, inflation has diverted savings from manufacturing investments to inflation hedges such as housing and speculative inventory holdings. All this must surely have increased the difficulty of expanding the nation's stock of plant and equipment.

There is little question, then, that for these and other reasons, inflation can be an enormous impediment to productivity growth. It follows that one of the major contributions government can make to stimulation of productivity is the adoption of fiscal, monetary, and other policies that promise to be effective in bringing the extraordinary inflation of the past decade to an end.

However, the preceding list of contributory causes still leaves us without a clear explanation. Why has U.S. productivity growth been *more* disappointing than that in other countries? Other countries suffered an oil shock more severe than our own. Others have regulatory programs that are as demanding as ours. In particular, it is noteworthy that rapid growth has occurred in countries that suffer from very high inflation rates, such as Korea and Brazil, whereas the United Kingdom had no inflation during its period of declining growth. Many foreign competitors in the growth race also have had an inflationary handicap, in some cases more onerous than our own. It is worth mentioning that the U.S. productivity slowdown began well before the 1970s and that, even before the onset of this inflation, our productivity growth rate had begun to lag far behind those of Japan and the leading industrial countries of Europe. Anti-inflation policy surely deserves a high priority, and nothing that has just been said should be construed to the contrary. But there is little basis for confidence that success on the inflation front is virtually all that is needed to solve our productivity problems.

PRODUCT QUALITY AS A COMPONENT OF PRODUCTIVITY

For increasing our international competitiveness and for benefiting the consumer, the quality of products is obviously an end in itself. In service industries, the quality of the service provided is crucial in determining both the level of productivity and the industry's international competitiveness.

Along with price, product quality has in recent years become one of the competitive weapons of the foreign producers who have been invading U.S. markets. Not so long ago, the label "Made in Japan" suggested a shoddy product, but now Japanese products are sought for their performance as well as their competitive price. The products of Germany, Sweden, and other countries enjoy similar reputations. It is clear that U.S. producers must be prepared to keep up with or exceed the product standards set by those countries if they are not to suffer serious marketing handicaps.

Because rejection rates are a significant element of quality in the production process, quality is quite literally an important component of productivity. All other things being equal, the lower a firm's rejection rate, the less its inputs are wasted, and hence the greater its productivity.

It is only slightly less obvious that if all other things are equal, the need for frequent repairs constitutes a deduction from productivity very similar to that caused by a high rejection rate, despite the fact that need for repairs is not taken into account in the standard productivity figures. If the production of two similar items uses equal quantities of labor but the first incurs negligible repair costs over its lifetime and the second requires many hours of attention, it is clear that the latter's ratio of value of output to quantity of labor will be far smaller (that is, that the productivity of its labor will be substantially lower). The need for repairs may have similar and more significant consequences for the productivity of capital equipment.

One study has found that "96 percent of [Japan's] automobiles leave the production line in fit shape for delivery, versus 75 percent of ours. American rent-a-car companies report that cars made in the United States require two to three times more servicing than comparable Japanese cars."[6]

It is certainly not fair to use such a small number of examples to condemn all American manufacturers. Nevertheless, these reports are consistent with widespread impressions about prevalent differences in quality. At best, they suggest that there is room for improvement in U.S. productivity through increased attention to quality.

Japanese industries that have significantly lower rejection or failure rates also seem to require significantly lower quantities of labor and other types of input (such as plant space and backup inventory). This strongly suggests that they have not achieved higher quality through disproportionate increases in the use of inputs. Quite the contrary, they seem to have managed their quality performance while using smaller input quantities.

---

6. Quoted by Peter G. Peterson, "The U.S. Competitive Position in the 1980s—And Some Things We Might Do About It" (Speech presented to the Center for International Business, Houston, March 1981).

Moreover, differences in performance do not necessarily stem from cultural differences. In the United Kingdom, for example, Japanese managers who operated a Sony plant using local workers quadrupled daily output of the plant and cut absenteeism to nearly a fifth of that in nearby British plants.[7] Of course, these figures are only suggestive. They omit the quantities, per unit of output, of indirect labor such as maintenance and management overhead, which, when considered, show Japanese performance to be less outstanding. What the overall differences in performance do suggest is that improvements in the performance of U.S. management can contribute significantly to productivity. To a very considerable extent, the fate of America in the international marketplace is in the hands of U.S. business leaders themselves.

---

7. Stephen Rattner, "Foreign Management Lessons: Sony Succeeds Where British Business Fails," *New York Times*, 14 December 1981, D1 and D2.

CHAPTER 5

PUBLIC POLICIES
FOR PRODUCTIVITY GROWTH

The market system's effectiveness in stimulating productivity will be substantially enhanced by the elimination of unnecessary government measures that now impede productivity and by the modification of public policies in ways that encourage investment for growth in future productivity. Government actions influence productivity in many ways—through their effects on the nation's capital stock, on the magnitude of basic research and applied R&D, and through their consequences for entrepreneurship. This chapter explores these relationships and provides a number of recommendations for public-policy changes that can contribute to productivity growth.

INCREASED INVESTMENT: THE PRICE OF GROWTH

An important conclusion that emerges from studies of the causes of the decline in our nation's productivity is that insufficient investment in plant and equipment is one of the major sources of the problem. As the labor force expands at a rate greater than the rate of investment growth, this reduces the amount of capital available per worker, impedes expansion in our nation's overall industrial plant, and condemns the U.S. labor force to relatively obsolete equipment and technology.

The rate of growth in capital investment (meaning non-residential, plant-and-equipment investment) is also important in explaining the differences between the U.S. productivity-growth rate and that of other industrial countries. Even if the United States increases its rate of investment, our competitors may continue to have much higher rates of increase in investment in plant and equipment. The share of our investment as a percent of output (gross domestic product) is about half as large as Japan's, and is much smaller than other industrial competitors'. During the 1970s, the United States increased its rate of capital investment in manufacturing, but other countries continued to invest a much larger proportion of the output of their economies in overall plant and equipment (Figure 8).

During the 1960s, Japan and West Germany had extremely high rates of investment. In the 1970s, the rates for both the total economy and manufacturing declined slightly for most countries, but the difference in rates of investment between the United States and other nations remained substantial. The consistently higher rates of capital investment by our competitors has contributed to their much higher rates of productivity growth (Figure 4, page 17). After twenty years, divergent productivity-growth rates have allowed other countries to match the productivity *levels* in some of our industries in a number of sectors of the economy.

Empirical studies of the causes of the productivity slowdown indicate that one crucial element in any promising productivity policy must be some set of measures that can markedly increase the share of productive investment in the United States. But no measure will be easy or painless. We know no magic that can double our investment rate overnight, and anything that does work will inevitably impose some sacrifices on particular groups or on society as a whole.

If a larger share of our nation's resources is devoted to investment, inevitably less will be left for other purposes. Some sacrifices will have to be accepted—in consumption, in housing, in entitlements, in military preparedness, or in something else—and, unavoidably, that will be painful to the groups affected. Only self-deception can support the belief that the nation can for any substantial period simultaneously expand its industrial plant, rebuild its roads and bridges, add to the rate at which its stock of houses grows, expand its military equipment, and increase the amount consumed by society.

Of course, an increase in industrial investment is not pure sacrifice. It does require us to give up current consumption or some other current outlay, but, in exchange, it promises increased consumption in the future as the expanded industrial capacity begins to yield its products. However, the

FIGURE 8

Average Annual Capital Investment as Percentage of Output (GDP)

	Total Economy		Manufacturing	
	1960–1969	1970–1977	1960–1969	1970–1977
Japan	28.8	26.7	29.9	26.5[a]
West Germany	20.1	18.7	16.3	15.2[b]
Canada	20.0	19.3	14.4	15.1
France	19.5	18.8	n.a.	n.a.
United Kingdom	16.5	17.6	13.4	13.6
United States	14.9	14.5	8.8	9.6

a. 1970–1974
b. 1970–1976
n.a.: not available

SOURCE: Committee for Economic Development, *Stimulating Technological Progress* (New York: CED, 1980), 23. These numbers are based on data provided by the U.S. Department of Labor, Bureau of Labor Statistics.

long-run consumer benefits of industrial investment—which are, of course, the ultimate purpose of such investment—must not blind us to the painful decisions that we must face today if productivity-growth policy is not to be foredoomed.

Increased federal support of research and development, changes in regulatory standards, modification of regulations that inhibit competition, and patent-policy changes that reduce the cost and delays imposed on business by current patent law are all desirable public-policy changes that can contribute to productivity. However, each individually is of only moderate significance. **This Committee believes that it is dangerous to assume that modest changes in one or two policy areas will be sufficient to reduce the gap in productivity performance between the United States and its competitors. We need a strategy in which significant changes are made simultaneously in a number of policy areas.**

STIMULATING SAVING AND INVESTMENT

An important share of the productivity slowdown of the 1970s has been attributed to limited investment, as has our relatively poor productivity performance. Studies indicate that the Japanese productivity phenomenon is explained to a large extent not by any unique cultural advantage, but by their much higher rates of saving and investment.[1] The U.S. government also places considerable significance on the higher rate of investment by Japanese business, especially before 1973, as a major factor in the outstanding productivity-growth rates achieved by the Japanese manufacturing sector.

If the United States wishes to retain its position as a leading economic power, it must be prepared to undertake striking departures from traditional policies. Disincentives to saving should be removed and the bias toward consumption created by tax and public-expenditure policies reduced. Steps must be taken to eliminate distortions that favor investment in types of assets unlikely to yield significant productivity improvements.

The stimulation of saving and the flow of investment resources to industry is clearly beyond the power of any private group within the econ-

1. J. R. Norsworthy, testimony on Recent Productivity Trends in the U.S. and Japan before the Senate Subcommittee on Employment and Productivity of the Committee on Labor and Human Resources (97th Congress, 2nd Session, 2 April 1982). Norsworthy estimates that from 1965 to 1973 the rate of growth in investment in manufacturing was about four times greater in Japan than it was in the United States. For an extensive review of the policy responses to poor productivity performance, see U.S. Senate, Committee on Labor and Human Resources, *Productivity and the American Economy: Report and Findings* (Washington D.C.: U.S. Government Printing Office, 1982).

omy. Although particular individuals or groups may save more as a patriotic gesture, it is hardly likely that such spontaneous acts can add up to a major upsurge in the national propensity. Yet, such an upsurge is surely required if this country is to have any hope of staying abreast of its competitors in the productivity race in terms of either capital-to-labor ratios or availability of modern and efficient types of capital equipment. Virtually all competing countries have rates of saving and investment in industry (calculated as shares of GDP) significantly above—sometimes twice as high as—the U.S. rate. It is in this area that government policy plays the key role. [2]

REDUCING THE CONSUMPTION BIAS AND THE DISINCENTIVES TO PERSONAL SAVING

During the postwar period, public expenditures have exhibited a strong current-consumption bias. In the 1960s, social transfers (transfer payments and grants-in-aid) increased 8 percent per year in real terms, and this average annual rate of growth in social transfers continued in the 1970s. In contrast, the real net rate of investment in public *capital* by federal, state, and local government—much of which is important for economic growth—declined from an annual rate of 3.8 percent in the 1960s to 1.8 percent in the 1970s.

We cannot be certain of the degree that tax incentives for home ownership are responsible for the investment that has gone into housing, but we do know that throughout the 1960s and 1970s, both the stock of residential capital and its rate of growth substantially exceeded those of manufacturing capital. The nation may place a high social value on home ownership and may not want to change that emphasis, but it should recognize that it has significant negative implications for productivity.

Over the last several years, saving has also been influenced by high inflation rates. People have begun to realize that the value of savings can be rapidly eroded by rising prices. Although the rate of inflation dropped sharply in 1982, it will take time for Americans to adjust their saving behavior to lower inflation. But the downward trend in inflation will contribute to higher saving rates in the future.

---

2. U.S. Department of Commerce, *Assessment of U.S. Competitiveness in High-Technology Industries* (Washington, D.C.: Government Printing Office, 1983). Throughout this report, much of the lack of U.S. competitiveness is attributed to insufficient U.S. capital formation. Insufficient investment by business occurs because managers feel the cost of capital is too high relative to its expected rate of return. The manner in which the government influences this cost is through fiscal policies. In addition, programs whose purpose is not directly related to the stimulation of investment also affect capital formation as government intervention in other areas spill over into the capital market. For example, the mix of monetary and fiscal policies to achieve noninflationary growth can affect the cost of capital. Similarly, interventions to restrict the return to individual savers can influence the supply of investable funds.

We believe that a number of direct policy changes are required if the saving rate is to come anywhere near the rates in other major industrial countries. The past policy of an interest-rate ceiling on savings accounts and government savings bonds at a rate well below the rate of inflation meant that small savings were virtually condemned by law to being eaten away by inflation. It is hardly surprising that most small-income earners have been disenchanted with the virtues of saving because of the fragile protection it seemed to offer. The complex of interest-rate ceilings on savings instruments most readily available to lower-income groups has been responsible for much of the inflationary loss small savers have suffered. Where the market for funds is free—that is, not impeded by regulation—interest rates will vary with the rate of inflation. Artificial impediments in the capital markets prevent compensatory adjustments in interest rates, and it is exactly these impediments that have been particularly damaging to lower-income groups. **We therefore support the elimination of legal impediments to interest-rate changes on small savings that has now occurred.**

In addition, the tax code should be modified to reduce the necessity for individuals to seek special arrangements to protect their earnings. The Economic Recovery Tax Act of 1981 has allowed for the deferral of the tax on individual savings until retirement, thus removing one of the disincentives to saving. In addition, the reduction in marginal tax rates should increase disposable income, and if this occurs, more should be saved. However, the magnitude of the effect on saving is difficult to predict because the tax cut that raised individual income has been accompanied by a decline in GNP, which will at least temporarily reduce the saving resulting from the tax reduction.[3] The tax-rate reduction may also produce some increase in the supply of work effort. For male workers, the incentive effect of higher earnings is likely to be much less than for women, whose work effort is much more sensitive to increases in earnings.[4] The responsiveness of women's work efforts to recent tax policy changes is likely to provide an additional source of higher levels of personal saving.

Excessive marginal tax rates, even at their recently reduced levels, are likely to have a detrimental effect on the work effort of a significant propor-

---

3. See Charles R. Hulten and June O'Neill, "Federal Tax Policies Under the Reagan Administration," in *The Reagan Experiment,* ed. John L. Palmer and Isabel V. Sawhill (Washington, D.C.: Urban Institute, 1982).

---

4. The Economic Recovery Tax Act has also reduced the marginal tax on married couples' earnings by reducing the so-called marriage penalty and increased the child-care tax credit.

tion of the American labor force.[5] Tax simplification can make an important contribution to productivity growth, even if the structure remains progressive. It can do so by reducing average and marginal tax rates through elimination of many special tax arrangements, and by reducing the debilitating influence of tax considerations upon personal and business decisions. **This Committee recommends that, at some future time, the tax code be reviewed with the intent of achieving substantial simplification in the structure of taxes, reductions in tax preferences, and reductions in marginal tax rates through a broadening of the tax base.**

TRANSFORMING INCREASED SAVING INTO INVESTMENT

Since 1973, the average annual rate of growth in gross capital investment, at least in U.S. manufacturing, has increased slightly. However, when depreciation of existing plant and equipment is taken into account, there has actually been no net increase in the rate of growth. The average annual rate of growth of net investment in *equipment* has declined slightly in real terms for both manufacturing and the overall nonresidential sector of the U.S. economy. This in itself is reason for concern, but the decline in the rate of investment in *plant* has been even more dramatic. The average annual increase in the net stock of overall nonresidential plant dropped from about 4 percent between 1960 to 1973 to 2 percent after 1973. For manufacturing plant, the figure declined from 1.6 percent between 1960 and 1973 to almost zero since 1973.[6]

This decline in capital investment is especially significant because an increase in productivity requires the availability of more and better plant and equipment. During the period 1960 to 1973, the plant and equipment provided each U.S. worker in the private sector increased at an average annual rate of 2.32 percent. Since 1973, the decline in the rate of capital investment, along with the rapid growth of the labor force, caused this rate to fall to 0.14 percent.

Investment in new plant and equipment is determined by expected demand and expected return as well as by tax policies that reduce the cost

---

5. Hulten and O'Neill, "Federal Tax Policies Under the Reagan Administration," 103. Over the 1960–1980 period, the marginal tax rate (excluding Social Security and state and local taxes) for a family of four with a median income rose from 20 to 24 percent. For families with twice the median income, it doubled to 43 percent. Over the next several years, the Economic Recovery Tax Act will prevent a further rise in these rates for some groups. For families with twice the median income, marginal rates will decline by several percentage points. However, median-income families will continue to have the same marginal rates as in 1980.

6. Calculations based on data from U.S. Department of Commerce, Bureau of Economic Analysis, *Survey of Current Business* (Washington, D.C.: U.S. Government Printing Office, April 1976 and August 1979).

of capital. Consumer demand and business capital can be "crowded out" by government spending financed either by increases in tax rates or by the issuance of bonds or tax-free securities. Consequently, the short-run influence of any supply-side tax reduction on the cost of capital can be overwhelmed by absence of demand growth, especially in a period of high real interest rates.

A major goal of the Economic Recovery Tax Act was to stimulate capital investment.[7] **This Committee strongly supports this tax policy change as part of any public-policy strategy to improve U.S. productivity growth. We also believe it is essential for the government to demonstrate that it can control federal expenditures and gradually reduce the budget deficit.** Unless this is done, the reduction in the effective corporate-tax rates achieved by the tax act may be insufficient to produce the consistently high level of investment in plant and equipment required for a significant long-run increase in productivity.[8]

Recent tax legislation has increased the incentive to save by permitting *all* wage earners to exclude savings from taxable income in IRAs, with the earnings on these accounts taxed on distribution. The annual maximum IRA deduction has also been liberalized.[9] Experience under the earlier IRA regulations suggests that this will gradually produce a large source of investable funds, thereby increasing the rate of capital formation.

The reduction in the highest marginal tax rate for individuals resulted in a decline in the maximum capital-gains tax rate of 8 percent; the rate went from 28 to 20 percent. However, the Economic Recovery Tax Act failed to remove the prime disincentive to investment during inflationary periods; income from capital continues to be taxed on the basis of *apparent* rather than *real* gains from investment. For example, if an individual had bought stocks in 1972 for $10,000 and sold them ten years later for $15,000, he would realize an apparent taxable gain of $5,000. If inflation during that period averaged 7 percent a year, this $15,000 would be worth

---

7. The concept of more rapid capital-recovery tax reforms incorporated in the new depreciation schedules in the Economic Recovery Tax Act was proposed in Chapter 4 of the policy statement *Stimulating Technological Progress* (New York: CED, 1980).

---

8. The Tax Equity and Fiscal Responsibility Act of 1982 was intended to reduce the projected growth in the budget deficit.

---

9. The new maximum deduction is $2,000 per worker ($2,250 for a couple with a single income) for IRAs, with a penalty for early distribution. The maximum deduction under Keogh Plans was also liberalized. These new incentives for saving are consistent with CED's previous recommendations. See Chapter 5 in the policy statement *Reforming Retirement Policies* (New York: CED, 1981).

only $7,500 in real terms (that is, in terms of 1972-dollar purchasing power), and the investor would have suffered a real loss of $2,500. If taxes were based on real gains and losses, the investor could report a real capital loss of $2,500, rather than paying a tax on an apparent $5,000 gain.

One approach that can achieve a degree of equity in the tax treatment of income from capital during an inflationary period is an adjustment in the value of the asset over the period it is held by deflating it with the aid of a standard price index such as the GNP deflator. Thus, for example, the investor would be recognized to have experienced a real capital loss of $2,500 rather than an apparent gain of $5,000. **This Committee recommends that some mechanism be adopted to adjust the valuation of capital gains for inflation and thereby eliminate a major impediment to saving and investment.***

Almost all funds for capital investment by corporations are now derived from retained earnings. Since these are less subject to the direct discipline of the market than funds raised externally, it is highly desirable to increase the share of investment funds raised in competitive capital markets. Removal of double taxation of dividends and control of inflation can do much to enhance the flow of funds from equity markets to productive investments.

DIRECTING INVESTMENT TOWARD OPPORTUNITIES FOR PRODUCTIVITY GROWTH

An effectively functioning market system is the most efficient mechanism for allocating capital and other resources to their most efficient use. Public policies can improve the operation of markets but should be designed to avoid or at least minimize distortions that favor investment in some types of assets and discourage it in others.[10] Complete neutrality in public policies is, of course, an unattainable ideal. Nevertheless, this Committee believes that policies that distort the operation of markets clearly inhibit growth in productivity, and should be modified.

The burden of taxation on saving should be reduced. The tax on individual contributions to Social Security and employer pension plans should be deferred from the time income is earned to the time retirement

10. The importance of sector-neutral policies and the minimizing of policy distortion will be addressed in the forthcoming policy statement on Industrial Strategy and Trade Policy.

*See memorandum by Richard M. Smith, page 93.

benefits are paid out.[11] This tax change should be gradually phased in to avoid inequities and to be consistent with the maintenance of budget discipline.

The public-expenditure bias against infrastructure investment must be reversed. In the United States, investment is needed to modernize and expand not only the capital equipment in the hands of private industry, but also the infrastructure capital in the public sector. During the 1970s, public expenditures favored present consumption over public investment. But the nation's roads, bridges, tunnels, airports, and other facilities are vital for the working of the economy; their deterioration can impede productivity and must be reversed. For example, efficiency in the work place will be significantly impaired if employees have to spend too much of their time coping with transportation facilities that are inadequate and unreliable. **We recommend a major increase in outlays for repairs, modernization, and expansion of the portion of the public infrastructure that contributes to productivity.** This will have to be phased in, both for the sake of efficiency and to reduce the effect upon the federal budget. These investments should be paid for, wherever feasible and appropriate, by user charges to prevent wasteful outlays and to assure payment of costs by those who benefit. Only in exceptional cases and with the most explicit justification should such costs be borne by the public treasury.

Public policy needs to be modified to ensure that investment incentives are neutral among types of capital assets. To achieve higher productivity-growth rates, it is necessary to reduce the cost of capital by allowing for quick recovery of investment in capital assets. In stimulating capital investment through rapid capital recovery, the taxation of income from that investment should be as neutral as possible, in the sense that the effective tax rates on income from different types of capital assets should be roughly similar. In the past, the investment tax credit has biased business investment in favor of equipment relative to plant. The effect of the Economic Recovery Tax Act magnified this bias; even though the act reduced the effective tax rate on income from new investment in both equipment and plant, the

---

11. This was recommended in the policy statement *Reforming Retirement Policies.* Admittedly, the immediate effects of such a tax change would be to raise the present after-tax disposable incomes of all workers paying into Social Security or private retirement plans with fixed in-payment rates, and these workers might spend rather than save most of this current gain. But over the longer run, this tax change would increase the net return to saving for retirement. Thus, employers would have a greater incentive to establish new or expanded pension plans with both employees and employers contributing to these plans. In the case of Social Security, the recommended tax change would increase the equity between generations of workers and retirees.

differential between the two actually widened from 16 to 33 percentage points favoring equipment.[12]

The new Accelerated Capital Recovery System and the changes in the Investment Tax Credit under the Economic Recovery Tax Act reduced the cost of capital to *all* industries. In the long run, this policy change is likely to contribute significantly to productivity growth. However, the effective tax rates for new investment in some industries were reduced much more than in others, so the dispersion of effective tax rates among industries was widened substantially.[13]

The Tax Equity and Fiscal Responsibility Act (TEFRA) of 1982 was adopted to restrain the substantial increases in the federal deficit. It also sought to modify somewhat the 1981 business tax reductions, which were mainly tax preferences affecting the new tax treatment of depreciation of some long-lived plant and the new investment tax credit provisions for some very short-lived equipment.

Over the years, various business tax preferences have been introduced into the tax code to promote particular goals thought to be desirable. Before TEFRA, it was estimated that losses in federal revenues through business tax preferences would rise from $48.8 billion in fiscal year 1981 to $188.0 billion in 1987.[14] As a result of TEFRA, this expansion is expected to be reduced significantly, mostly because of changes in provisions on investment tax credit (a reduction in the amount of the credit that can be used as an offset to tax liabilities, for example) and the repeal of the new declining-balance method of depreciation, which was to go into effect in 1985.

Since the Investment Tax Credit and the Accelerated Capital Recovery System are two of the most substantial business tax preferences, TEFRA has eliminated the negative effective tax rates on new capital investment that were available to some industries before its passage. Consequently, the range of disparity in effective tax rates among industries is narrower in comparison with that under the 1981 tax act; TEFRA has thereby produced a more neutral system of taxation of business income.

---

12. See Hulten and O'Neill, "Tax Policies," 112.

---

13. "Effective Corporate Tax Rates in 1980," *Fortune,* 18 October 1982, 144. Indeed, it is estimated that under the Economic Recovery Tax Act, the new effective tax rates among industries varied in 1981 from -12.6 percent to about 40 percent. See *Tax Notes,* 11 October 1982, 159.

---

14. For a discussion of the conceptual and technical difficulties in estimating the revenue loss, see *Redefining Government's Role in the Market System* (New York: CED, 1979), 46. Despite these difficulties, the projected growth of the revenue loss from these preferences was substantial under the Economic Recovery Tax Act of 1981.

The 1981 and 1982 tax acts in combination are a significant stimulus for the productivity growth that can be expected as we recover from the recent recession. However, effective tax rates on new capital investment still vary among broad industrial categories and the differences probably are greater than they were before the Economic Recovery Tax Act. Some misallocation of capital resources will continue and could partially offset the stimulus to productivity growth stemming from the general reduction in tax rates on new capital investment.

New investment in capital assets may continue to flow more readily to industries with the most favorable tax treatment. This would mean that the overall growth of the economy could be impeded as too much investment flows to some industries and not enough to others.

It is important to examine ways in which the tax system can be made more neutral. One way would be to permit "expensing," that is, permitting the cost of equipment and plant to be deducted at the time of purchase. This would avoid the allocation of assets among separate depreciation-rate categories, which is a major source of the current bias.[15] Another area to examine is business-tax preferences, some of which are potential sources of interindustry distortions in the allocation of capital resources. For example, an investment tax credit with rates that differ by type of equipment can result in some bias among industries. There is general agreement, however, that under an "expensing" system, the investment tax credit is unnecessary, and might even result in negative tax rates on returns to new investment. If the remaining business tax preferences, though aimed at stimulating economic activity, are retained along with "expensing," distortions in investment will still occur. Such preferences that apply to particular industries constitute a disincentive to investment in other industries. Designers of future tax policy should consider the trade-off between a reduction in the large number of particular business tax preferences and a substantial reduction in the corporate rate.[16]

---

15. Allocation of assets among depreciation categories will be neutral only if the depreciation rate for assets in each class is exactly equal to the economic life of the asset, and if the rates take into account both inflation and the replacement cost of the asset. Any attempt to calculate the economic life of assets in real terms is rejected because of the enormous difficulties in administration and estimation. In contrast, some form of expensing would avoid administrative difficulties and at the same time achieve the goal of more rapid capital recovery for all industries.

---

16. The possible percentage-point reduction of the corporate rate from the current statutory rate of 46 percent will depend on the estimated revenue loss of tax credits and preferences, which are traded off for the corporate rate reduction. It may be possible, eventually, to reduce the statutory corporate rate perhaps to the 25–30 percent range if many tax arrangements for business, other than "expensing," were eliminated. In the short run, however, the potential percentage-point reduction is likely to be quite modest because the current schedule of deductions for existing capital would have to be retained at the same time "expensing" for new capital would be introduced.

A move toward an expensing system of capital recovery is only one approach to reducing tax-policy distortions. Other approaches should also be considered for an overall program to increase productivity. In choosing among such options, it is important to recognize that making changes in tax policy temporarily introduces uncertainty in investment decisions. Consequently, in designing a more neutral tax policy it is important to minimize the short-term dislocations that any new approach inevitably involves.

STIMULATING TECHNOLOGICAL CHANGE

The invention, development, and introduction of new techniques for producing goods and services are critical sources of long-term productivity growth. Using growth in research and development expenditures as an indicator of technological change, most studies conclude that a slowdown in R&D growth accounts for between 10 and 18 percent of the U.S. decline in productivity improvement since 1973.[17]

Government policy affects the rate of innovation stimulated by the market mechanism in a number of ways. The government has always been the main source of funds for *basic* research. Individual firms have little incentive to invest in basic research because its returns are rarely retainable by the enterprise that undertakes it. In addition, the long lead time generally associated with the return on investment for basic research makes this use of capital unattractive for most corporations.

In contrast, for research that is intended directly for *commercial application*, the market system offers companies the incentive to invest without direct government intervention, provided that patent policy permits enterprises to profit from their R&D outlays. Government regulatory and tax policies should be designed to minimize disincentives to research and development and to promote the growth of new and innovative firms. Finally, because research outlays involve a much higher risk and a much longer payoff period than other forms of investment, incentives that are available to all firms equally may contribute to long-term productivity growth in the market economy.

POLICIES FOR INVESTMENT IN BASIC RESEARCH

In recent years the costs of basic research have been rising rapidly. Many research projects in the physical and biological sciences require long periods, sizable and frequently interdisciplinary research teams, increasingly sophisticated instrumentation, and special facilities. Moreover, gov-

---

17. See Edward N. Wolff, "The Magnitude and Causes of the Recent Productivity Slowdown in the U.S.: A Survey of Recent Studies" in *Stimulation of U.S. Productivity Growth*, ed. William J. Baumol and Kenneth McLennan (forthcoming).

ernment regulations related to the environment, health and safety, and the use of human and animal test subjects have added to these costs.

Basic research is by no means financed exclusively by the federal government; industry, private foundations, private-university endowments, and state-university budgets are also important sources of funds. Nevertheless, because it is difficult for private investments to capitalize on the results of basic research, there is no realistic alternative to the federal government as the primary source of money. **We urge that the government explicitly adopt as a major national objective a consistently high level of support for basic research.** We believe that in the long run, consistent, stable financial support will provide the country with a strong base of knowledge for future economic growth and industrial innovation.

In much government-supported basic research in universities, a complementary relationship exists between the performance of basic research and the education of engineers and scientists. Those who train engineers and scientists must have contact with the frontiers of knowledge; that is what it means to conduct basic research. In addition, education of graduate students depends on their active involvement in research projects. **We believe that the federal government should increase its funding of basic research, especially in universities, even at the cost of other activities.** The effectiveness of government funding for basic research at universities can be increased by the following measures.[18]

- **Government should pay the full cost of research performed under contract by universities.**

- **To encourage the development of high-quality researchers, government should finance individual scholars of outstanding ability rather than invest equally among a large number of institutions.**

- **The sharing of high-cost instruments among universities should be encouraged whenever that will contribute to the return on research investments.**

The employment of these principles in the support of research in the basic academic disciplines is best left primarily to the National Science Foundation and other federal agencies that finance such research. The widely used system for allocating research funds based on the review of

---

18. For a more extensive discussion of these guidelines, see *Stimulating Technological Progress,* Chapter 7.

proposals by other scholars has generally served the country well. This system can perform even better if agencies are held accountable for the broad character of the research they support, rather than for the individual projects they choose.

In an attempt to assist basic research at universities, the tax credit for the donation of certain research equipment in physical and biological sciences has been liberalized under the Economic Recovery Tax Act of 1981. We support this tax change because it should lead to improvement in the quality of basic research and in training of researchers at universities by contributing to the sophistication of their equipment, and should help them to meet their instrumentation needs. Universities and business should seek ways in which they can increase cooperation in the support and conduct of basic research.

POLICIES FOR INVESTMENT IN RESEARCH WITH COMMERCIAL APPLICATIONS

Government's role in research and development aimed at commercial applications ought to be restricted to broad-based indirect incentives designed to take advantage of the inherent efficiencies of the market system.* However, this principle still leaves several areas in which the government can properly play a more direct role in the financing of research and development.

- **Direct federal uses.** The government has a role to play in the design and financing of innovations intended primarily for public-sector activities such as defense, space exploration, mail delivery, air traffic control, and regulation. Indeed, about 15 percent of the defense budget consists of R&D activities.

- **National priorities.** Health, environmental protection, and agriculture are among the areas in which the government has made a commitment to research and development. A broad-based tax incentive to private activity will not elicit the same amount of R&D activity in all sectors of the economy. For example, in industries such as agriculture, firms may be too small to undertake research and development, even though valuable new information and ideas can be obtained at a modest cost.

Aside from these areas, tax regulations can also be amended to reduce disincentives to R&D outlays by private companies. CED welcomes the temporary suspension of the Treasury Regulation 1.861–8 since its tax treatment of R&D expenses encouraged some industries to perform their R&D abroad.

---

*See memorandum by Philip M. Klutznick, page 94.

If the measure is reintroduced, we urge that it be changed so that only the portion of a U.S. parent company's R&D expenses directly related and traceable to foreign earnings be treated as a deduction from foreign-source income.

The potentially significant stimulus to R&D through the tax credit for incremental increases in R&D investment in the 1981 tax act is a desirable policy change (see "Recent Policy Changes to Stimulate R&D," opposite). This is, however, only a temporary program. When experience under this incentive is evaluated **we recommend that the government consider the introduction of a flexible system of depreciation of R&D capital assets by extension of Section 174 to permit the expensing of R&D structures and equipment.** This would make the U.S. tax treatment of expenditure on R&D equipment more comparable to the favorable treatment it receives in Japan and other industrial nations.

A number of recent patent law changes should help stimulate innovation (see "Recent Patent Changes to Stimulate Innovation," page 62). It is unfortunate, however, that current patent and tax laws discriminate against technology transfers. A serious disincentive to such transfers, particularly in times of rapid inflation, is the requirement that expenditures for purchased patents be capitalized and depreciated on a straight-line basis over the useful life of the patent, which may be as long as seventeen years. For the acquisition of other types of techniques such as unpatentable proprietary processes or know-how for which there is no generally accepted useful lifetime, the purchaser cannot deduct any part of the acquisition cost. The requirement that such expenditures be capitalized, compared with immediate expensing of costs for internally developed technology, discourages the purchase and dissemination of improved techniques and limits the market opportunities of inventors. Economic growth and efficiency are penalized when these tax disincentives cause newly developed techniques to lie fallow while businesses that could use these techniques productively in their innovation activities expend valuable resources to reinvent the wheel. In order to eliminate the resulting uncertainty and to encourage innovation, **we believe that the government should consider permitting firms to write off expenditures for the purchase of patent rights or other externally designed innovations.**

A number of recent tax changes are likely to encourage the establishment and expansion of small, innovative firms. These changes include a reduction in the corporate tax rate, lower taxation of capital gains, an increase in the number of shareholders permitted in Subchapter S corpora-

RECENT POLICY CHANGES TO STIMULATE R&D

The government recently introduced two temporary tax-policy changes that directly affect some business R&D decisions. One minor change for the better has been the two-year suspension of Treasury Regulation 1.861–8.

Before its suspension, this regulation required multinational corporations with headquarters in the U.S. to allocate a portion of their R&D expenses to their income from foreign sources even when that R&D was performed entirely in the United States. Consequently, the regulation raised the worldwide taxes paid by U.S. corporations that receive a high proportion of their total earnings from operations in foreign industrial nations with high tax rates. It also encouraged some U.S. corporations to conduct much of their research in other countries in order to receive the full deduction of R&D expenses.

The government has also made the concept of an incremental R&D tax credit part of the Economic Recovery Tax Act, providing for a credit equal to 25 percent of the increase in qualified tax expenditures over a base period. This incremental credit will be available from June 1981 to December 31, 1985. For 1981, 1980 serves as the base period for R&D expenditure; for 1982, the base period is the average of 1980 and 1981 outlays. Thereafter, a three-year-average base period is used.

The intangible expenses generally include wages, supplies, lease or other charges for computers, lab equipment, and up to 65 percent of contract research. It is also possible to carry forward unused R&D tax credits up to fifteen years. This latter feature of the credit is likely to be beneficial to investment in research that will not yield a profit for a long period of time. It will also be helpful to new firms entering R&D-intensive industries.

There may be some imperfections in the design of the incremental tax credit. R&D equipment is assigned to a three-year asset class for depreciation, but it receives only a 6-percent investment tax credit. Equipment would normally have fallen into a five-year class, in which it would be eligible for a 10-percent tax credit. It is therefore not clear that firms will gain from the new credit. Experience under this temporary provision remains to be evaluated.

62

tions from fifteen to thirty-five,[19] removal of impediments to use by small firms of last-in, first-out (LIFO) inventory accounting, and the availability of favorable tax treatment of stock options to employees of small enterprises. Such stock options should be especially important for growth in small, innovative firms because they can be used as a form of compensation in the

---

19. In *Stimulating Technological Progress*, CED recommended that in the future an extension of the shareholder limit to 100 for Subchapter S corporations is desirable. This change will increase the availability of capital to new firms by eliminating the taxation of dividends received by shareholders investing in small corporations.

RECENT PATENT CHANGES TO STIMULATE INNOVATION

In a market economy, property rights in the results of successful research must be protected by an efficient patent system if adequate investment in research and new production techniques is to occur. In the policy statement *Stimulating Technological Progress* (1980), we recommend a number of changes to increase the effectiveness of the patent system and strengthen its supportive role in the innovation process. CED advocated establishment of a single court of appeals for patent cases to provide nationwide uniformity in the patent law. In addition, we proposed a reexamination procedure, that, at the request of parties other than the patentee, would permit the Patent and Trademark Office to strike obviously invalid patents from the rolls. The policy statement also advocated that voluntary arbitration should be endorsed by statute as an acceptable way of reducing the cost and time required to settle patent controversies. The Committee is pleased that all of these proposals have recently been enacted into law.

The timing of the patent grant is crucial for its role in business planning. Here, two changes are important. First, to give adequate protection to innovation in fields subject to government regulation, **a procedure should be established providing an appropriate adjustment in the patent term when commercialization is held up because of regulatory delay.** Second, to prevent extended controversies and long delays in the issue of patents when two or more inventors claim the same improvement, **the nation should change to a first-to-file system, whereby the first inventor to file a patent application will receive the patent.** (A personal right of use can be preserved for anyone filing later who in fact invented first and took steps leading to commercialization.) Under such a system, the ownership of all patents would be determined promptly, and the public would benefit from early publication of the patent disclosure.

early years, when the short-term payoff from the research and development and capital investment is likely to be quite small. This committee believes that these policy changes are worthwhile.

REMOVING UNNECESSARY REGULATORY IMPEDIMENTS

Government regulations that constrain economic behavior in minute detail can be a critical impediment to growth.[20] But such restraints alone are not fully responsible for the productivity problem. Most of the European economies whose productivity growth has persistently and significantly exceeded ours have been able to do so despite a great deal of social regulations. In contrast, the United Kingdom's prime period of relative decline, from 1870 to 1914, was also an era in which its businesses were virtually unregulated. Nevertheless, the evidence suggests that increased regulation is responsible for perhaps between 10 and 15 percent of the slowdown in U.S. productivity growth during the 1970s.[21] Unnecessary constraints on the market system raise private costs of production and discourage the productivity improvement that competitive markets stimulate. Thus, although deregulation alone is unlikely to restore U.S. leadership in productivity growth, the reduction of such restraints will contribute to its revival.

One purpose of government regulation of industry is protection of the public interest from monopoly power, which impedes the operation of the market system. Regulation for this purpose is referred to as *economic* regulation to distinguish it from *social* regulation, which seeks to protect health, safety, the environment, and other objectives of public concern. Economic regulation—of pricing, investment, market-entry decisions that companies usually control—is designed to limit what some consider an unacceptable amount of market power. Even where such intervention was originally justifiable, as it may have been in the case of the railroads before the emergence of trucking, it has become indefensible in cases where market power has been eroded.

Many observers have concluded that in a good number of industries economic regulation no longer has a useful purpose, and that a substantial

---

20. CED addressed the problems of government intervention in the economy in *Redefining Government's Role in the Market System* (New York: CED, 1979).

---

21. See Wolff, "The Magnitude and Causes of the Productivity Slowdown in the United States: A Survey of Recent Studies."

degree of deregulation will serve the public interest. **We therefore recommend that the government press forward with economic deregulation in areas in which effective competition is no longer absent. Many markets served by public utilities and by the trucking, railroad, and air-transportation industries now meet this test.** The partial deregulation of railroads should continue and any moves toward partial de facto re-regulation should be resisted. The recent partial deregulation of telecommunications has undoubtedly passed the point of no return, and it is difficult to justify continuation of full regulation of the industry's major enterprises in the presence of unregulated entrants that are growing rapidly in number and size.

Traditional public-utility regulation has prevented utilities from earning revenues sufficient to attract the capital they need for expansion and modernization. It has forced capital to remain in activities that do not pass the market test and therefore make no economic sense. It has delayed decisions and caused unnecessary lags in response to changing market and technological conditions, and it has inhibited the exercise of entrepreneurship. It has distorted prices and thereby led to misallocation and waste of resources. For all these reasons, **it is essential that the heavy social costs of public-utility regulation be recognized in cases where it yields only marginal benefits and that regulation be eliminated wherever the real social costs exceed the real social benefits** (taking into account both costs and benefits that are not reducible to dollars).

In a market economy there is good reason for an antitrust program that stimulates competitive behavior. However, the primary consequence of some antitrust measures has been a weakening of competition by protecting less successful and less efficient enterprises. In addition, uncertainty in the interpretation of antitrust policies may have inhibited many businesses from engaging in joint ventures that could have increased the efficiency of production and contributed to the competitive strength of American enterprises. Inconsistency between U.S. antitrust policies and those in other countries may well have inhibited international activities of American firms. **Therefore, we urge policy makers to review current antitrust policies, particularly in light of increased world competition, and consider modification of any antitrust laws that inhibit productivity growth rather than stimulate competitiveness in the international market.**[22]

---

22. Specific recommendations on antitrust policies will be presented in the forthcoming CED policy statement on Industrial Strategy and Trade Policy.

REDUCING THE COST OF REGULATORY GOALS

If the market system does not provide adequate information to consumers and other market participants, or if, as in the case of environmental pollution, detrimental consequences of production are imposed on society, some form of government involvement is justified. Moreover, it is important to recognize that the protection of the consumer, the environment, and the safety of the workplace have produced many benefits. When properly designed, such measures have contributed materially to the quality of life and the welfare of the community without interfering unduly with the efficiency of production.

Although this Committee recognizes the appropriateness of regulations controlling the undesirable side effects of production, we believe that many such regulations have been adopted without adequate weighing of their costs and benefits. Standards have often been decided upon more or less arbitrarily, and there is good reason to believe that some regulation has been carried well beyond the point that the public welfare can justify. Moreover, many regulations have cost the economy far more than necessary for the attainment of their goals.

A number of actions could be taken to reduce the costs of meeting desirable regulatory goals while permitting more effective use of the nation's productive resources by reliance on the sort of incentives that are central to the operation of the market system.

For example, zero-risk regulatory goals are rarely attainable, and the closer that goal is to realization, the greater the associated rise in social costs. Some of the most extreme advocates of social-benefit regulation argue that human life, health, and the nation's environmental resources are beyond price and that, accordingly, any measure that protects any of these is desirable no matter what it costs. Moreover, they maintain that cost-benefit analysis is inherently impossible to carry out because so many benefits are difficult to observe and still harder to quantify. What they fail to realize is that zero pollution, absolute safety in the workplace, and perfect information are unattainable. The question is not whether the atmosphere will contain particulates or the waterways some waste, but just how much of these pollutants it is in the overall social interest to eliminate. They do not recognize that as one nears the unrealizable goal of zero emissions, successive increases in purity become increasingly and prohibitively costly. Most of all, they fail to understand that the costs in question are not "mere money" but, rather, real resources that can have a high price in terms of foregone social opportunities elsewhere. In the allocation of effort and resources, society must constantly make choices and reevaluate priorities among equally legitimate social goals. The amount of labor and steel used to construct an excessively costly effluent treatment plant cannot be used elsewhere; that means it is no longer available for the construction of schools, hospitals, concert halls, or new plant and equipment needed to raise the nation's quality of life. Scarcity of the nation's resources may then make it appropriate to forego small steps toward one social goal if it threatens to inhibit significant progress toward another.

Accordingly, we urge that social-benefit regulations be subjected to cost-benefit tests on the basis of information that is relevant and reasonably attainable. It may be that some standards are not severe enough and that increased regulation and enforcement are called for. For example, this may be true for the disposal of highly toxic wastes. But where the severity of current regulatory standards fails the cost-benefit tests, action should be taken to reduce their unjustifiable burden on the economy and its productivity.

The use of absolute regulatory requirements and direct controls should be avoided wherever possible; appropriate regulatory goals should be pursued primarily through market incentives. All too often regulatory techniques have been designed in a manner that maximizes their interference with freedom of economic decision making and increases their administrative and other compliance costs. Firms are, in effect, told how to select their raw materials, equipment, and plant location. The interpretation and administration of volumes of detailed legislation and regulation make compliance enormously expensive and often render it all but impossible.

Much of this is neither necessary nor defensible. Recent innovative measures instituted by the Environmental Protection Agency, including the *bubble concept* and the *offsets program* (see "Principles of the Bubble and Offsets Programs," opposite) have demonstrated how environmental benefits can be attained with a far lower cost of resources and much less inhibition of freedom. Unfortunately, in practice these programs have been impeded by administrative provisions that have unnecessarily limited their flexibility.

Economists have long advocated the use of financial incentives rather than detailed and inflexible regulations as the least costly and least onerous way to achieve social goals. If social-purpose regulation is not to act as an unbridgeable impediment to productivity growth, it is certainly essential that every available means be used to increase its flexibility and reduce its

PRINCIPLES OF THE BUBBLE AND OFFSETS PROGRAMS

The *bubble* concept is designed to permit a company to choose not only the technological details of the means by which it meets assigned emission targets but also the processes and the plants from which these reductions are obtained. The concept assumes a "bubble" over an entire operation with an overall standard set for whatever various components within the "bubble" emit. For example, a firm that is expected to reduce its emissions of sulfur dioxide by 10 percent is not told whether to achieve it by installing smokestack scrubbers or switching to fuel with a lower sulfur content. If it has three plants operating side by side, it is not told to reduce emissions from all three plants proportionately. If it is cheaper to install very effective purification equipment in plant A, leaving plants B and C to operate just as they did before, the firm is permitted to do so, provided that its overall emissions targets are met.

Clearly, this approach can give management far greater freedom of choice than traditional regulatory procedures do. Moreover, by not interfering with decision processes, this approach permits management to select the least costly and most efficient means to comply with the standards.

The *offsets* approach permits managements even greater freedom of action. (This is also true of a later version of the bubble concept.) Suppose that factories A and B, owned by different firms, are side by side and that both are required to curb emissions of some pollutant by ten tons a week. Suppose also that for plant A, the cost of such reduction is $20 a ton; whereas for B, it is only $5 a ton (because its plant is more modern or because its product permits greater flexibility). Under the offsets approach, plant A is permitted to continue its original quantity of emissions if, say, by paying the owners of plant B $10 per additional ton of emissions reduction, it induces B to cut its emissions by the full twenty tons required of the two plants together. In this way, firms are left free to use the market mechanism to allocate the task among themselves in the manner that is mutually least costly, and is therefore likely to be least costly to society. Unfortunately, so far, the use of these approaches has been restricted in its application to new plants and the current arrangements have severely limited interfirm trades of the sort just described.

costs. Experience with the financial-incentives approach and with imaginative programs such as the bubble and offsets concepts, when carried out in a reasonable manner, demonstrate that such improvements in the regulatory mechanism are possible. It is urgent that their use be extended to whatever degree is feasible.

The bubble concept is now being introduced on a case-by-case basis. Although over 100 permits utilizing variations of this approach have been approved by the Environmental Protection Agency, only a few are actually in operation. **This Committee urges the government to simplify and accelerate rapidly the process of approval of the use of the bubble and offsets programs.** Moreover, it must be recognized that the fullest cost-saving and other benefits from such approaches can be attained only if new as well as old capital equipment are subjected equally to their provisions. **New as well as old plant and equipment should be eligible for inclusion in the bubble and the offsets programs.** Current attempts to improve environmental-control technology through government standards for engineering designs, together with exclusion of new plant and equipment from such programs, impose a heavy cost on society. In the interest of both productivity improvement and the protection of the environment, **we recommend that new source performance-standard regulations, which now restrict the inclusion of new plant and equipment in the bubble, be modified by amending the enabling legislation to permit more general use of the innovative bubble concept.**

The market system works through its penalties for poor economic performance as well as through rewards for successful activity. Regulatory policy can benefit from an analogous approach, using a system of financial incentives, rather than an enormous number of detailed regulations. Pricing incentives, such as effluent fees for waste discharges and excessive noise levels, can make excessive pollution unprofitable and provide a strong incentive for business to seek the least costly means to achieve the regulatory goal.[23]

FEDERAL RESEARCH AND TECHNOLOGY-ENHANCING PROGRAMS

The effectiveness of the market system in enhancing productivity growth depends on the availability of reliable information on economic performance in all sectors of the economy. In recent years, the Bureau of

---

23. CED has long opposed the use of detailed regulatory design standards and advocated use of the "polluter pays" principle wherever feasible. See *Redefining Government's Role in the Market System,* 102–197, and *More Effective Programs for a Cleaner Environment* (New York: CED, 1974).

Labor Statistics has extended its program of international comparisons of productivity growth and unit-production costs, and has designed a total-factor productivity index for manufacturing. **We commend these improvements in the U.S. statistical series on productivity and urge that the new total-factor productivity measure be published as a regular statistical series for individual industries as well as the entire private economy.**

The design of productivity policy can benefit significantly from improved productivity statistics for the nonmanufacturing sectors of the U.S. economy as well, since the output of the service sector represents a significant proportion of our GNP. Although this Committee recognizes the technical problems involved in taking quality changes into account and the difficulty of measuring the intangible outputs of services such as health care and education, especially in many of the service sectors, **we believe it is essential that the government improve the quality and coverage of data on productivity trends in services such as transportation, utilities, trade, finance, and insurance, to make the information comparable with that for manufacturing.**

In addition, the U.S. General Accounting Office has estimated that in fiscal year 1980 more than $2 billion was spent by federal government programs to fund research, improve and maintain productivity measures, transfer technological developments, and aid private-sector productivity in other ways. Although the government has a pervasive effect on the nation's productivity performance, there has been little success in coordinating the numerous productivity-related programs or in assessing their effect on productivity. There may be need for a focal point for attention on productivity-related activities within the federal government that would provide direction, coordination, and evaluation of government productivity policies and programs. These efforts can help keep productivity issues in the forefront of other economic policy making.

THE COMPLEX BUSINESS-GOVERNMENT RELATIONSHIP

The relationship between business and government is an intricate one, and at times, the nature of the relationship itself complicates government's influence on productivity performance. For example, government regulation of business activity has made it necessary for management to divert substantial energy and resources into dealing with regulatory matters and away from productive investment. But at the same time, many businesses and industries feel they have much to gain by regulation, and campaign against deregulation.

While businesses frequently rail against government interference in the market system, many also urge government to protect them against foreign and domestic competition, to raise protective tariffs, or to use antitrust laws and other means to gain advantage. Others are increasingly litigious and quick to use the government-provided judicial process to stifle competition. These and other legal and administrative aspects of the business-government relationship reduce the impetus for innovation and improved productivity.

There are several policy implications that emerge from the aspects of the business-government relationship that interfere inappropriately with business decision making and that divert vital resources away from productivity activities.

- Regulations whose costs exceed their benefits should be eliminated.

- Social-regulation programs—such as environmental-protection programs—should be redesigned so that benefits are achieved with minimal cost and minimal interference with business decision making.

- Government should not interfere with the market system's penalties for poor business performance. In particular, it should avoid special assistance to individual firms or industries.

- Management itself will have to reduce the frequency with which it takes recourse to courts and to government agencies and it should look more to the marketplace for help in achieving business objectives.

These changes can contribute to the efficiency of American management and stimulate the exercise of entrepreneurship so important·to future productivity growth.

CHAPTER 6

WHAT MANAGEMENT AND LABOR CAN DO

However great the importance of proper government policies, and however significant the changes in overall circumstances to which business must adapt, the critical role in productivity performance is played by business management, which makes most of the decisions on the country's production of goods and services.*

If management can increase the quantity and yield of capital available to the firm, invest effectively, deploy assets more appropriately, manage the work force more efficiently, and adapt the product line more promptly while reacting efficiently to government regulations, business fluctuations, and energy and raw material constraints, it will simultaneously improve the firm's long-run profitability and its productivity performance. The more effectively management carries out these tasks, the more productivity can be increased, both in individual companies and in the nation as a whole. The converse is also true; indeed, poor management can dissipate much of the opportunity for increased productivity that can be provided by the changes in governmental policy recommended in Chapter 5.

Of course there will always be great variations in productivity performance among companies and industries depending on size and type of firm and stage of product life cycle. For example, faster depreciation of plant

*See memorandum by Franklin A. Lindsay, page 93.

and equipment for tax purposes provides greater relief to capital-intensive firms, and an improved patent system will probably be of special value to research-oriented firms in fields characterized by particularly rapid technological change.

Time can also make a difference in the importance of productivity considerations in management decisions. In the day-to-day battle for sales and for market position, productivity growth may often be subordinated to objectives that bear fruit much sooner. Most significant productivity advances take considerable time—often years—to conceive, introduce, and carry out. But in the long run, a firm's productivity performance is a crucial component of its ability to survive and prosper. With few exceptions, each company will become, at some point, vulnerable to competitors whose productivity-growth rates are consistently higher than its own. Sooner or later, the competitors' growing advantages will translate into new sales—which, for the original company, mean some sales are lost. Because such a change in relative productivity position is usually a gradual process, some managements and unions may be lulled into underestimating the consequences. This kind of misjudgment can be particularly insidious where most of the competitors are foreign. Dramatic examples of the consequences of underestimating changes in foreign companies' relative productivity are now front-page news as the trading world grows more interdependent. Private enterprise now has ample reason to recognize that success in achieving productivity growth maintains and enhances the kind of competitive advantage that determines not only compensation and profits, but also—eventually—the survival or disappearance of whole categories of product lines and jobs. *Companies must constantly match the productivity levels of leading competitors if they are to retain their economic leadership.*

Many firms have not taken full advantage of opportunities for internal promotion of productivity growth. But others have, and this chapter provides examples of companies that successfully use particular productivity-improving techniques. Our purpose is to call attention to such opportunities, which may be overlooked in the day-to-day operation of many a business. (See "Guidelines: Incorporating Productivity-Enhancing Techniques into Management Process," opposite.)

STRATEGIC TOOLS FOR PRODUCTIVITY GROWTH

A large array of productivity-stimulating techniques is available to managers. Because each organization, company, and industry has its own set of priorities and problems, the optimal set of techniques will vary from firm to firm. Consequently, we cannot recommend that any particular approach or package of techniques should be adopted by all managements. Nevertheless, a general characterization of the available methods can facilitate and, we hope, encourage their use. Techniques that enhance productivity can usefully be divided into two categories: *strategic*[1] and *operational*.

Strategic decisions about introduction of new products or major redesign of production processes can bring quantum leaps in productivity.

---

1. For further discussion of this subject, see Michael H. Moskow, *Strategic Planning in Business and Government* (New York: CED, 1978).

GUIDELINES: INCORPORATING PRODUCTIVITY-ENHANCING TECHNIQUES INTO MANAGEMENT PROCESS

- Productivity growth is an issue that is important for a company's strategic plans, and therefore it should be assigned an explicit role in the strategic planning process.

- Entrepreneurship is one of the keys to productivity growth and is important for both large and small enterprises. Its stimulation requires explicit steps to encourage risk taking, departures from standard procedures, and the presence of individuals who deviate from routine and standard-behavior patterns in a creative manner.

- Effective organization and execution of productivity programs require the design of appropriate indices to measure a company's productivity performance and that of its leading foreign and domestic competitors. This information should be available to all levels of management.

- In selecting techniques for the promotion of productivity, management must not make its decisions piecemeal. Rather it needs to choose a set of measures constituting a *balanced portfolio* in which the methods selected complement one another and promise to deal effectively with all the major productivity problems facing the enterprise. It is equally important for management to attempt an explicit evaluation of the potential sufficiency of the selected portfolio for the achievement of overall productivity objectives.

- Like the rest of the work force, management needs to be motivated to devote the effort and attention required for attainment of long-run productivity goals. Linking promotion and compensation directly to productivity changes can elicit significant contributions from middle management.

Strategic planning may embody technological advances, adaptations of product design based on buyer needs, or conservation of energy or materials. But most of what planning promises rests on the appropriate *timing* of these strategic decisions, and timing, in turn, requires foresight. Inevitably, it takes a long time to identify technological changes that are feasible commercially, to adapt plant and equipment to such changes, and to stimulate market receptivity to a new or significantly redesigned product.

STRATEGIC ANALYSIS

The first step toward strategic analysis is characterization of the technological and market environment in which the company will operate and recognition of the importance of productivity for its competitive position. This requires monitoring of pertinent technological developments in the firm's own laboratories, elsewhere in the industry, and in the relevant university facilities. Such developments not only must be *identified* but also *evaluated*.

U.S. multinational corporations recognize that strategic analysis must encompass both domestic and foreign competitors. Other kinds of companies are also gradually recognizing that the internationalization of markets should be taken into account in their strategic-planning process. Industry trade associations may be helpful in establishing innovation-analysis units in major industrial countries that can monitor technological developments and report them to their members.

The experience of most innovative firms demonstrates that strategic analysis needs to extend far enough into the future to provide indications about future markets in which a company will have to sell the outputs of its still-unbuilt plants. For many firms, that period of analysis may be five years, ten years, or even longer. Although longer projections are inevitably more conjectural, it still is necessary for a firm to make the best possible estimates. Companies must at least look as far ahead as their domestic and foreign competitors do.

Strategic analysis varies greatly among firms. Large organizations may undertake extensive formal programs. They will then be faced with the problem of communicating the relevant information to all of their decision-making groups—something that may be less complicated for smaller enterprises. Small firms usually have to rely on much more informal methods, and could be helped a great deal by well-designed productivity-scanning programs provided by industry trade associations. **Although the choice of particular techniques must be adapted to the needs and capabilities of the organizations involved, every American business firm and industrial asso-**

ciation will find it useful to review its program of strategic and productivity analysis and revise it when necessary to assure it is adequate to meet the competitive challenges before it.

STRATEGIC RESPONSE

A key difficulty is the communication of strategic challenges to those who are in positions to respond effectively, and have access to the requisite time, talent, and capital. The innovative approach of Westinghouse Electric Corporation shows how productivity analysis can constitute an important component of strategic response (see "Productivity and Strategic Planning at Westinghouse," page 77). But whichever approach is taken, it is important that it not underestimate future productivity gains that can be realized through proposed innovations in products and processes. In particular, firms should avoid the error of comparing anticipated rates of return on productive investments calculated in *real* (that is, inflation-adjusted) terms with costs of funds or discount rates expressed in *nominal* terms.

Recognizing that the choice of specific techniques must be adapted to the needs and capabilities of the individual firm, we recommend that every American business adopt explicit productivity goals that it considers adequate to meet its competitive challenges now and in the future.

FORMULATING OPERATIONAL PRODUCTIVITY GOALS

Three primary reasons have been suggested to explain why many firms have not taken full advantage of opportunities for internal promotion of productivity growth.

- Absence of adequate internal measures of productivity performance or of similar information about competing foreign and domestic firms and industries.

- Difficulty of setting target values against which the firm's performance data can be compared.

- Lack of a reliable internal market mechanism that can provide the incentives to elicit from middle management significant contributions to productivity that are likely to involve some risk and disturbance of current practices.

The very lack of clear productivity measures within companies and industries can frustrate efforts to alleviate the national productivity problem. Techniques for stimulating productivity are available to management, but many firms lack appropriate long-range measures to guide their decisions.

The improvement of statistics on international productivity performance for individual industries is important in helping industry management understand how their own performance relates to the magnitude of the productivity problem that faces the nation. A target for the rate of growth of national productivity is of no use as a goal for an individual industry because each business is different. However, since managements within each industry face similar decisions on technology, manufacturing processes, product design, and marketing constraints, estimates of average productivity trends in their own and competing industries both at home and abroad may provide a useful basis for developing the operational goals required to improve the firm's productivity performance.

We recognize that transnational comparisons of productivity levels are extremely difficult. Nevertheless, unless U.S. businesses have some information about the trends in total-factor productivity and input prices in the foreign industries with which they compete, they risk eventually losing their ability to compete. And this problem is not confined to manufacturing firms. A higher rate of productivity growth in some types of service industries in other countries can gradually induce loss of market share for corresponding U.S. service firms that currently enjoy a cost advantage because of their superior productivity.

Executives who have the requisite information will be in a position to design appropriate measures for their own industries. In fact, driven by the pressures of international competition, some industries or even individual companies have already constructed useful measures that may well be suitable for others.

Trade and professional organizations and industry publications may wish to create and encourage productivity-stimulating programs. Such programs could include preparing publications that increase awareness of the productivity issue and sponsoring seminars and specially designed courses in the techniques already adopted by firms within the industry.

ENTREPRENEURSHIP: THE BASIS FOR ACHIEVING PRODUCTIVITY GOALS

Entrepreneurship is the ability to perceive and seize opportunities, to act boldly, decisively, and innovatively in unfamiliar terrain. Entrepreneurship can take credit for much of this nation's enviable record of innovation. But it has been said that in recent years the spirit of entrepreneurship in our

PRODUCTIVITY AND STRATEGIC PLANNING
AT WESTINGHOUSE

In 1979, Westinghouse Electric Corporation intensified a corporation-wide program for productivity and quality improvement. A strategic plan was developed to encourage employee participation in identifying and solving job-related problems. Westinghouse also launched technological activities to improve productivity performance.

For each of the businesses in the corporation, it established specific productivity-improvement objectives in terms of annual increase and constant-dollar value-added per employee. The overall corporate-productivity objective is a 6-percent improvement in productivity per year. By using a simple productivity measure in constant dollars of value added at the organizational-unit level, it is measuring the productivity of both its blue- and white-collar workers. In its Public Systems Company, Westinghouse has exceeded the corporate objective, achieving an increase of 7 percent during each of the past three years, and Public Systems is striving for a 10-percent increase per year.

Westinghouse's Vice President of Corporate Productivity, a newly-created position, assumes full-time responsibility for extensive productivity-improvement efforts and manages a Corporate Productivity and Quality Center. This center brings together many of the productivity- and quality-related support activities, and includes an extensive manufacturing-technology development laboratory. A corporate productivity committee was also organized and a dozen subcommittees were established to bring together top experts of its line operations, to help decide corporate direction, and to help other operations launch analogous programs. Among the subcommittee titles are Organizing for Productivity, Quality Circles (see page 84), Value Engineering, Robotics, Computer Aided Design, Computer Aided Information and Control Systems, and New Plant Programs.

The productivity committee also administers a multi-million-dollar "seed money" fund that is available to all Westinghouse operations with a minimum of paperwork. The fund is now generally aimed at high-risk, high-payoff projects that have potential applications in a number of corporate locations. About $40 million has been committed to about 200 projects.

SOURCE: Thomas Murrin, paper presented before the Productivity Panel of the Economic Policy Council, United Nations Association of the United States of America, 4 February 1982.

country has flagged. Clearly, removal of impediments to entrepreneurship will provide a major stimulus to the health of the economy.

Entrepreneurship is frequently associated with small, newly founded businesses. Such firms have often introduced revolutionary new products and innovative, productive techniques. Consequently, it is essential that impediments to the establishment and entry of new firms be avoided assiduously.

However, large firms have made their share of contributions to economic change, and they, too, are in need of entrepreneurs, whose role, unlike that of routine management, is to introduce innovation, prevent stagnation, and modify procedures as needed.

The immediate hallmark of an entrepreneur is that he disturbs the comfortable routine of his more conservative colleagues. He can be expected to point out inefficiencies and inadequacies in current procedures and to introduce new and disquieting methods and ideas. Thus, although it is easy to pay lip service to the desirability of entrepreneurship, organizations are apt to restrict or even impede the activities of entrepreneurial types, or even to avoid hiring them. If it is to flourish, it is important that the spirit of entrepreneurship should be instilled and encouraged from the very top. Without leadership and determined commitment of resources by top management, the entrepreneurial side of the business is likely to languish as time passes.

Even if management intends to encourage entrepreneurship, the organizational bureaucracy within large companies may drift into the adoption of rules and customs that quarantine entrepreneurs down the line. The box on page 79, based on corporate experience, may help management to recognize when a firm has adopted such a pattern inadvertently.

CHOOSING A PORTFOLIO OF PRODUCTIVITY-STIMULATING TECHNIQUES

Discussions of particular operational techniques for enhancing productivity tend to focus on individual devices, such as quality circles or robotization. Each of these techniques, in appropriate circumstances, promises a real contribution. However, adoption of such approaches because of current fashion, or random selection of a few of these approaches, is not usually the most advantageous route to take.

Rather, top management can make its most important contribution by choosing the *portfolio of techniques* best suited to its circumstances.

- Management needs to recognize that its productivity goals can normally be attained only by a *balanced portfolio* of measures that complement one another and are sufficiently diversified to cover all of the productivity problems of the enterprise. Excessive attention to the latest in "progressive" management is likely to prove disappointing and inadequate.

- Top management should evaluate its entire portfolio of productivity-enhancing measures to determine if the program is *sufficient* to attain the company's overall productivity goals.

In practice, a productivity program is often not evaluated according to its promise of sufficiency. If each of the techniques included in the company portfolio is judged to be practical and desirable in itself, management is all too likely to be satisfied with the overall program. Only explicit consideration of sufficiency can enable management to recognize when its plans have gone far enough to offer a reasonable degree of assurance that its goals will be realized.

**ENCOURAGING ENTREPRENEURSHIP
WITHIN THE ORGANIZATION**

- *Risk.* Does the company encourage middle- and lower-level management to take reasonable risks? How does it reward success? Does the penalty for failure inhibit innovation?

- *Recognition of Innovators.* Does the firm go out of its way to recognize the accomplishments of innovators? Do they regularly attain status in the company commensurate with their contribution?

- *Availability of Avenues of Innovation.* Are there easily accessible avenues along which innovators can have their ideas evaluated and put into practice? Are they likely to be blocked by internal bureaucracy? Is access to top management readily available to them?

- *Organized Provisions to Encourage Innovation.* Has the firm considered such organizational arrangements as small subsidiaries or special divisions, in which innovation is encouraged and within which specially selected individuals can operate effectively?

- *Encouragement of Constructive Criticism.* Are there provisions for rewarding individuals who point out inefficiencies, defects in current operations, and other types of poor business practice? Or are such persons apt to be fired, isolated, or punished in other ways?

OPERATIONAL TECHNIQUES TO IMPROVE PRODUCTIVITY

Most productivity-enhancing techniques relate to four broad areas: technological choices, including R&D and innovation; the deployment, use, and replacement of capital equipment; the contribution of company personnel; and resource allocation to higher productivity endeavors.

Many firms have recently shown interest in new approaches to the management of the work force. A wide range of programs that encourage and motivate employees is already being adopted by some companies. The diversity of these programs is suggested by the following list of categories into which they can be classified.[2]

- *Building values.* This is accomplished either by hiring workers whose values are compatible with the objectives of the organization or, when that is impossible, achieving the same result by suitable training of workers.

- *Making jobs more attractive.* This includes both improvement of physical working conditions and redesign of work groups and jobs.

- *Setting goals for managers, individual workers, and work groups.*

- *Supporting effectiveness.* This can mean extra training, skill development, quality circles, and the like.

- *Rewarding performance.* Income-sharing plans, performance appraisals, and other reinforcement systems would be in this category.

- *Improving the quality of working life.* This is the newest approach, and includes participative management, sociotechnical systems, and the entire science of organization development.

Although managers at all levels sometimes believe that workers lack motivation and are interested only in their paychecks, research in industrial psychology and sociology since the 1940s clearly demonstrates that such a broad generalization is unfounded.[3] Perhaps as a response to poor productivity performance and loss of competitiveness, many U.S. firms are

2. This discussion is largely based on Robert B. McKersie and Jan Klein, "Productivity: The Industrial Relations Connection" in *Stimulation of U.S. Productivity Growth,* ed. William J. Baumol and Kenneth McLennan (forthcoming), and on an unpublished study (1981) by R. D. Katzell and D. Awal of New York University.

3. For a review of the early research on this issue, see Frederic Herzberg et. al., *Job Attitudes: Review of Research and Opinion* (Pittsburgh: Psychological Service of Pittsburgh, 1957). Since 1950, many researchers, including Robert Dubin and Rensis Likert, have demonstrated that in particular organizational environments, workers do respond to more extensive responsibilities in work situations and wish to participate in the determination of organizational goals and their achievement.

beginning to take the results of this research into account in their own organizational planning. Although these private-sector initiatives will rarely produce spectacular improvements, **we believe that top management should review and introduce new approaches to work organization to encourage the entire enterprise—workers *and* management—to participate in activities that improve productivity.**

Workers have a vital interest in increasing productivity in their own organizations. In the final analysis, employment security depends to a significant degree on continuous growth in output per worker. In the past, workers in some industries have attempted to achieve some degree of job protection though collectively negotiated provisions covering crew size, the division of work among relatively rigid craft boundaries, and restrictions on management's ability to deploy labor among occupations.

Job-protection provisions, which frequently emerge from free collective bargaining, can be an impediment to long-run productivity growth. In a few industries, labor and management are beginning to recognize that both can benefit by avoiding such restrictions. Productivity bargaining and the use of labor-management committees whose task is improvement of productivity have been important parts of the collective bargaining process in some recent negotiations. Too often, however, there is not enough emphasis on modification of growth-inhibiting provisions. **We therefore urge that management and workers in all firms reconsider any work rules that inhibit productivity growth.** Joint labor-management productivity activities need to extend beyond current collective-bargaining developments, which in most cases seek primarily to modify the rapid increase in wage and compensation packages that were adopted in the late seventies.

If the firm has unions, it is essential for those unions to be involved substantially and explicitly in all productivity-enhancement programs affecting its members. This may require a new attitude on the part of management and union leaders alike. *It also requires that the union leaders and union members fully recognize that failure to meet competition through improved productivity will inevitably result in loss of employment or curtailed growth in wages or both.* For its part, management must carry out compensation and employee-participation programs that motivate the work force and reward employees for their contribution to the organization's productivity performance.[4]

Experience has shown that there is no one ideal approach. Evaluation of individual projects is made more difficult by the interdependence of the many steps that are taken to improve productivity. For instance, trying to improve work-force motivation without simultaneous examination of the

---

4. For further discussion, see McKersie and Klein, "Productivity: The Industrial Relations Connection."

materials, equipment, tools, and systems that the work force uses will undoubtedly do little more than increase frustration for all parties.

Experience also indicates that productivity-improving mechanisms should be well planned and tailored to the specific needs of the company. Slavish imitation of models from other companies or other countries is likely to bring disappointing results. In this respect, it is worthwhile to note that Japanese companies generally deny that they employ any rigidly defined or standard management programs. (See the appendix, "Successful Economic Policy in the Far East," page 95.)

If labor is invited to participate in problem solving, it is essential that the involvement be real and substantial. Cosmetic participatory programs are all too likely to backfire, producing nothing but lasting resentment and suspicion. In addition, we believe that it is appropriate for workers, as well as for investors and management, to expect tangible rewards for demonstrable contributions to the prosperity of the firm.

To involve all participants in an enterprise in the pursuit of a common goal remains one of the most difficult challenges any organization faces. But it is also one with which almost everyone in the enterprise can identify. From the myriad techniques available, we have chosen several to illustrate the options some companies are exercising.

GAIN-SHARING SYSTEMS

Gain-sharing systems enable workers to share directly in the increased income that comes from improvements in the activities of their group. Gain sharing is different from profit sharing, which awards the worker a proportion of *total* company profit. Some observers feel that the effectiveness of profit sharing is likely to prove to be limited because the individual worker in a large company will probably feel powerless to influence the overall earnings of the firm to any noticeable degree, and because company profits are affected by so many external factors (such as exchange rates) that are entirely beyond the worker's control.

The form in which gains are shared with the group may vary considerably from firm to firm. Some businesses may simply elect to give the workers shares of the gains for which they are responsible in the form of cash. Others may provide improved fringe benefits. Still others may choose forms of recognition that involve no financial element, although one may well be skeptical about the long-term effectiveness of such an approach.

A number of companies in this country have adopted a Scanlon Plan for gain sharing. Developed by Joseph Scanlon, the late official of the United Steel Workers of America, these plans are designed to give employees an incentive to improve production methods and suggest cost savings. For a Scanlon Plan to be successful, it is crucial to establish a network of production committees that involve everyone in productivity improvement; the organization must also be able to measure the difference between plant output and total payroll cost for the reward system. For details about one company's experience with a Scanlon Plan, see "Improving Productivity Through Employee Incentives at Dana Corporation," below.

IMPROVING PRODUCTIVITY THROUGH EMPLOYEE INCENTIVES AT DANA CORPORATION

Dana's Scanlon Plan has been used in twenty-two of the corporation's plants (approximately one-third of the major facilities), and it involves approximately 5,000 people.

Each department has a *production committee* consisting of three or four employees, with their supervisor serving as chairman. The committee solicits and evaluates suggestions, and, on average, 75 percent of the suggestions submitted are accepted and carried out.

Some suggestions have resulted in substantial savings. At one plant a test engineer suggested using a new process that has resulted in a projected saving of $875,000 a year in a particular production operation.

Cash rewards are computed from historical data and measurement of the ratio between plant output and total payroll. The ratio is used to estimate the allowable payroll each month. If the actual payroll is less than the allowed payroll, three-fourths of the difference is distributed to the employees as bonuses and one-fourth is retained for future investment in capital equipment. At the end of the month, all employees receive the same percentage bonus. Typical bonuses for a plan average 15 percent, with the range being from zero to 30 percent.

Dana reports that in 1971, the year before it first used the Scanlon Plan in its U.S. plants, its North American sales were $636 million, and monthly employment averaged 24,300. Ten years later, average monthly employment had increased only slightly, to 25,600, but North American sales had almost quadrupled to over $2.2 billion. Even after adjusting for inflation, annual sales per employee during this period nearly doubled, from $23,300 in 1971 to $43,000 in 1981. (For more information about the Dana Corporation, see page 87.)

SOURCE: Robert A. Cowie, testimony before the Subcommittee on Employment and Productivity, Senate Labor and Human Resources Committee (97th Congress, 2nd session, 2 April 1982). For further information, see also U.S. Senate, Committee on Labor and Human Resources, *Productivity in the American Economy: Report and Findings* (Washington, D.C.: U.S. Government Printing Office, 1982).

As a special form of gain sharing, management may wish to consider direct rewards to those responsible for suggesting innovations that make major contributions to company profits.

- Since General Motors instituted its suggestion plan in 1942, North American employees have submitted more than sixteen million suggestions, over four million of which have been adopted. GM estimates that suggestions have been responsible for measurable cost savings of up to $1.34 billion during their first year of use. Actual savings have been much higher since most continue to accumulate savings two to three years after adoption.

  Awards paid represent one-fifth of the net first-year savings and range from a minimum of $25 to a maximum of $10,000. In 1981, 167 employees received maximum awards.

  GM stresses that a highly professional approach, with emphasis on real and tangible savings, and strong support by both line supervisors and top management are essential to successful management of any suggestion plan.

QUALITY CIRCLES

Quality circles are voluntary worker groups that meet periodically (often weekly) to discuss what can be done to increase productivity in their areas of activity. Widely used in Japan, quality circles tend to focus on improvements the workers themselves can carry out. Japanese experience suggests that such groups have been most effective when they were formed on the workers' initiative, rather than imposed from above.

Quality circles may improve job satisfaction, reduce absenteeism, improve product quality, or generally increase the efficiency of output. In some cases, productivity improvement has been management's primary goal in instituting a companywide system of quality circles.

- As part of its intensified overall effort to improve productivity, Westinghouse Electric Corporation has formed about 1,500 quality circles involving 15,000 employees at over 200 locations. All the quality circles have made some positive contribution, and some circles have identified problems and developed solutions that have been worth between $500,000 and $1,000,000 per year in cost savings.

TOTAL WORK SYSTEMS

Whereas the quality-circle approach treats employee participation as an adjunct to normal work responsibilities, the total-work-systems approach treats it as an integral part. "Open systems" or "sociotechnical systems" are two examples of this approach. Under such systems, employees are trained to perform a range of tasks and become involved with problem solving and decision making. Participation in setting goals, making budgets, and other processes formerly viewed as the exclusive domain of management is also expected. In most cases, employees coordinate activities among themselves and with other organized units. Employee work groups or teams become largely self-directed, releasing management energies for productive use elsewhere. The development and efficient functioning of these new work systems require extensive training and communication. They also require new types of reward systems, both monetary and nonmonetary, based primarily on skill acquisition and employee contribution to the performance of the business. The new work systems produce employees who are multiskilled, flexible, well-informed, and highly committed; their energies are more clearly focused on how their productivity affects the business.

Substantial resources and a long-term commitment on the part of corporate management are necessary for such a program to stand a reasonable chance of success. Management must genuinely understand the crucial value (even necessity) of channeling employee talent toward business objectives, recognize the hard work involved, and begin the task of changing outmoded traditional managerial attitudes about the role of working men and women.

LABOR-MANAGEMENT PARTICIPATION TEAMS

Management may find it useful to establish labor-management participation teams to involve workers in deciding how to solve operational and production problems. Both Bethlehem Steel and the Ford Motor Company have undertaken such labor-management problem-solving activities.

- In 1980, Bethlehem Steel entered into an experimental agreement with the United Steelworkers of America to establish Labor/Management Participation Teams at selected plants. The teams, which are organized around work units, usually include seven to thirteen employees and supervisors. Each team tries to identify and solve problems that relate to performance, morale, dignity, and conditions of the work site. Subjects a team might discuss include use of production facilities, product quality, the work environment, safety, environmental health, scheduling and reporting arrangements, absenteeism, overtime, job assignments, contracting out, energy conservation, transportation pools, and incentives for more efficient use of resources.

As of 1982, over thirty teams are functioning in five Bethlehem plants. Although they are relatively new, some teams have achieved notable successes. One team achieved a 50-percent reduction in scrap by devising a system that made use of short lengths of stock material that would previously have been discarded. Another team designed procedures that reduced bent (unusable) steel bars by 80 percent.

While difficult to measure, Bethlehem reports that there is a significant improvement in overall communication, cooperation, and worker-supervisor relationships in locations where teams are functioning. [5]

- In 1979, the Ford Motor Company and the United Auto Workers agreed to launch the UAW-Ford Employee Involvement process. Today, over sixty Ford locations (including virtually all major facilities) have Employee Involvement Projects in operation. Some 800 separate employee problem-solving groups are functioning, involving nearly 10,000 employees.

Many of the problem-solving groups have devised innovative approaches that have improved work environment, product quality, and productivity. Ford views the program as a major contributor to its 48-percent product-quality improvement in two model-years.

As an example, Ford cites the effectiveness of the program at the company's Dearborn Glass Plant where a new glass oven was needed. The lowest bid from an outside manufacturer was $800,000. Plant management consulted the problem-solving groups to determine whether they could build the oven at a more reasonable cost. The result: the employees built the oven from scratch for less than half of the lowest bid and delivered it a week before deadline.

In addition to measurable benefits, Ford says there are other benefits from Employee Involvement. Plants with such programs are consistently characterized by better communication, improved shop-floor harmony, increased employee satisfaction, better labor-management relationships, and fewer grievances. [6]

PRODUCTIVITY-TRAINING PROGRAMS

A company may consider establishing special voluntary training programs to teach new and more productive skills to employees. These programs can provide necessary retraining and cross-training to protect workers from skill obsolescence and can increase opportunities for ad-

---

5. This information was provided by the Industrial Relations Department of the Bethlehem Steel Corporation.

6. This information was provided by the Industrial Relations Department of the Ford Motor Company.

vancement. While retraining has been important for high-level skills in such areas as science and engineering, rapidly changing technology has made retraining essential for workers at all skill levels. But the productivity-training programs will prove effective only if the worker has the opportunity to benefit from the new skills.

- In 1969, Dana Corporation established Dana University to train its employees in supervision, cost-control management, and sales and marketing. Division and plant management select the students and courses, and pay tuition and other expenses. In 1981, nearly 2,300 people participated in seventeen courses.

  Dana U also coordinates a regional program that brings training to all 35,000 Dana employees at reduced cost. Out of 104 U.S. plants, 86 conduct their own courses with the help of the regional program. (For more information about the Dana Corporation, see the box on page 83.)

EMPLOYMENT TENURE

Some managements may find it useful to consider the adoption of a limited scheme of formal employment tenure. In much of American industry, a form of job security through seniority has long been accepted. To be sure, such seniority protection has not extended to the entire work force of U.S. companies, but that is also true of the oft-heralded employment tenure practices in Japan. Japanese employment tenure is limited to 40 percent or less of the labor force, usually workers at large corporations. However, the fact that workers in key positions, who represent a substantial portion of the firm's work force, are publicly granted a special and stronger form of job security means that new productive techniques will not constitute a threat to them but will increase the prosperity of the firm. The ease with which Japanese management has been able to introduce new technology may well be partly attributable to their employment-tenure system. The same may be true of the Israeli kibbutzim, whose members are never threatened with the loss of their employment and whose productivity-growth record has substantially exceeded that of the rest of the Israeli economy.

To be most efficient, employment security should not be organized in a way that forms a barrier to shifts in the allocation of resources in response to changes in market conditions or the evolution of technology, and so must involve flexibility in job assignment. Workers whose employment is guaranteed must be prepared to change both the nature of what they do and the location at which they do it, if necessary. They must be prepared to accept reassignment and retraining should the need arise.

We wish to emphasize that we are not urging universal adoption of a system of job tenure. However, **we do believe that an individual company's decision to offer more employment security can be a useful part of a productivity portfolio if it is accompanied by broad flexibility in assignment and retraining of workers.** For their part, workers should realize that the cost of providing employment tenure may quite legitimately require some offset in future increases in wages and other improvements in the benefit package. It is important to stress the significant role of management's authority in reassigning tenured workers; without such flexibility, employment tenure is likely to impede productivity growth.

MANAGEMENT INCENTIVES

We believe that substantial improvements are possible in the overall performance of management. In discussions of American productivity performance, it is frequently alleged that U.S. management is excessively oriented toward the short run. This is sometimes contrasted unfavorably with the situation in other countries. In this light, it may be worthwhile to consider a careful review and possible restructuring of the compensation arrangements for top-level management. Some observers believe that the way compensation is now structured emphasizes contributions to short-term performance and induces relative neglect of longer-term interests.

Executive compensation constitutes only one of the sources of incentives to management. For example, there is evidence that prospects for promotion provide stronger motivation than the immediate compensation arrangements. Similarly, pride in the enterprise and personal involvement in its success are undoubtedly prime stimuli to managerial dedication and effort.

Nevertheless, in an economy that is heavily dependent on the profit motive, compensation as well as promotion is surely an important consideration. All this suggests that incentive payments to management may be most effective if they are tied to some combination of current and future company profits, perhaps based on a moving growth average of a five-to-ten-year period, rather than on current profits alone. Care should be exercised, however, to calculate profits in real economic terms rather than by conventional accounting procedures (see "Do Conventional Measures of Long-Term Profit Effectively Reflect Productivity?" page 89). One rearrangement of this sort involves deferment of bonuses based on profit sharing (with suitable interest payment to compensate for the delay) so that the reward of the current management can be based to a greater extent on the actual future performance of the firm.

Ninety-five of the one hundred largest U.S. industrial companies currently provide some form of long-term executive compensation. If a company finds that its long-term incentive plans fail to elicit an adequate long-term orientation, it may mean that they need to be redesigned to reward pursuit of both financial and nonfinancial goals. Or, payments awarded under performance-based plans may need to be tilted more toward long-run achievements. In the 1970s, many companies espoused a "pay for performance" philosophy of incentive compensation. Effective as those plans may have been in focusing attention on financial achievement, many organizations now want to direct executives' efforts toward long-term strategic objectives to increase the current real value of the enterprise to its owners.

DO CONVENTIONAL MEASURES OF SHORT-TERM PROFIT EFFECTIVELY REFLECT PRODUCTIVITY?

In a competitive market, true economic profit is a good indicator of productivity. Management's accomplishments, on the other hand, are often evaluated in terms of earnings per share, return on investment, and profit margin. If accounting figures like these were always a satisfactory measure of true economic profits, then they would be a reasonable index of management's productivity performance.

Unfortunately, at least in the short run, the two types of profit figures often differ significantly. The most important reason is inflation. If the accounting process is not adjusted for inflation, the accounting profit figure is likely to be a substantial overvaluation of true economic profits. When, for example, the rate of inflation is 10 percent, an accounting profit rate of 16 percent of sales represents a net economic profit rate of only 6 percent, the remainder simply constituting compensation for the erosion of the purchasing power of the stockholders' investments.

There are other reasons why accounting and economic profit figures usually diverge. For example, the expected yields of investment in research and development may be realized only in the distant future. These returns do not enter into the short-run financial flows that appear in current company accounts. Other widely discussed approaches, such as capitalization and expensing, can also distort accounting profit figures.

It follows that if the primary guide for management compensation is short-run profitability as measured in the accounting records, the resulting signals for decision making are likely to be distorted and the ensuing pattern of incentives is likely to serve neither the long-run profitability of the firm nor the long-run productivity goals of the economy.

The vast majority of short-term executive-incentive compensation plans base their awards almost exclusively on annual growth in profits or a related measure that reflects the quality of these profits, like return on assets or return on equity. Most long-term incentive plans are designed to reward executives for increases over time in the price of the company's stock (through stock options or stock-appreciation rights) or for improved earnings per share or return on assets (through related performance incentive plans). More recently, programs like performance share plans or combination stock-option and performance-unit plans have been used to reward executives for both market-price appreciation and the achievement of selected financial results.[7] Specifically, such arrangements can include:

- *stock-appreciation rights,* meaning a right granted in connection with an option whereby the executive, instead of exercising the option, can be paid the amount by which the fair market value of the stock exceeds the option price. Payments can be made in cash, in shares of stock having an equivalent value, or both.

- *performance share awards,* which are a contingent grant of company shares that can then be earned by meeting established performance goals within a certain period (usually three to five years). The executive may receive payment in shares, the cash equivalent of those shares (where they are equal), or a combination of cash and stock of equivalent value.

- *performance unit awards,* which are reward units earned by meeting established performance goals over a certain period, usually three to five years. The company is free to assign a monetary value to these units, and payment is usually made in the form of cash, company stock, or a combination of the two.

In summary, if a management-compensation plan is oriented primarily to short-term financial results (that is, the annual budget), executives will be strongly tempted to give only superficial attention to the execution of tasks that have long-range strategic and financial implications. Executive incentive compensation plans that seek to reinforce strategic objectives should support and be consistent with a comprehensive-performance management system that identifies the business strategies necessary to achieve the organization's mission, prepares an annual operating plan specifying the objectives and steps by which the strategies are to be carried out, and rewards executives for both the execution of the strategic plans and the financial results that follow.

---

7. This information was provided by the international management consulting firm of Towers, Perrin, Forster & Crosby.

CONCLUDING COMMENTS

Several broad conclusions emerge from this survey of what companies can do to contribute to the nation's productivity.

- There is a great deal that companies can do to initiate productivity improvement strategies.

- The measures that are most effective will vary enormously from company to company, and that is precisely why no single approach can be systematically described, nor can a small set be definitively recommended.

- Encouragement of entrepreneurship within the firm requires an entrepreneurial leader and a firm commitment, not merely good intentions.

- Top management can render maximum service to productivity growth by adoption of a portfolio of complementary techniques valued explicitly for their promise of sufficiency in achieving the company's objectives.

- Companies need to keep careful watch on the productivity of their foreign and domestic competitors and will have to rest content with no less than parity of performance if they are to achieve adequate protection of their own interests and those of the country as a whole.

It is clear that if the United States is to remain a leading industrial power through the next decade—and for the foreseeable future—its productivity-growth rate must at least match the rates of other industrial nations. On the basis of the current productivity performance of our competitors, this means we must substantially exceed the highest rates we achieved in the 1950s and 1960s. If we fail in this task, the country is virtually certain to be condemned to reduced international economic status by the end of the century and a lower relative standard of living. The current state of the economy of the United Kingdom, once the world's undisputed industrial leader, shows that such things can and do happen. Today, the United Kingdom has declined to the point where the real income of the average worker is between one-half and two-thirds of that in leading European economies.

Such a scenario for the future real income of the American worker is by no means out of the question; in fact, current trends point in that direction. This scenario brings with it the prospect of increasing competitive difficulties in the international marketplace for industries where productivity performance is poor. It also portends an inability to protect the living standards of large segments of the population (such as the elderly), an inability to reduce poverty, and a shortfall in the pursuit of a variety of other social goals. In fact, it threatens to constrain the standard of living of the entire labor force and their dependents.

It may be, as some say, that the fault in the United States is a decline in the spirit of workmanship and entrepreneurship. But even if this is true, surely that spirit only lies dormant and it can be reawakened. Both public policies and private measures by management and labor can contribute dramatically to the efficiency of every sector of the U.S. economy. With the restoration of the appropriate incentives and with the adoption of measures that are sufficiently bold and imaginative, we can be confident that the nation will rise to the challenge once again.

MEMORANDA OF COMMENT, RESERVATION, OR DISSENT

Page 2, by Roy L. Ash

This statement provides some very useful information and insights that can help those who are dealing with America's productivity problems. However, the analytical treatment of the information gathered and the absence of other relevant data and reasoning leaves an unconvincing case for some of the conclusions reached and recommendations made. Although I agree with many of the recommendations, I believe a number of them stand (in this document) independent of supporting evidence and argument.

Page 6 and 71, by Franklin A. Lindsay, with which Rafael Carrion, Jr., Philip M. Klutznick, J.W. McSwiney, and Elmer B. Staats have asked to be associated

I would like to underline a major conclusion of this statement that industrial management bears the responsibility for improvement in productivity. Statements in the past by many organizations have tended to lay such responsibility at the doorstep of others, mainly labor and government. While both do bear major responsibility, it is appropriate that CED, whose members are primarily top corporation executives, should identify the quality of management decisions as key to improving productivity.

Page 53, by Richard M. Smith

The U.S. economy would be better served by eliminating federal income tax on investment capital gains from individuals. While indexation of gain from a single form of financial asset might appeal to a given constituency, others may prefer to index different assets. Total indexation would appear to be a disincentive to political control of inflation.

Page 59, by Philip M. Klutznick, with which Elmer B. Staats has asked to be associated

While applied research is essentially the domain of the private entrepreneur, there may be situations in which it is important to reduce the time gap between basic research and applied research, or where the situation may be of such size in terms of financial outlay that appropriate provision should be made for either a collaboration between the government and the private sector, or else for segments of the private sector to be permitted to cooperate in a given situation among themselves.

APPENDIX
SUCCESSFUL ECONOMIC POLICY
IN THE FAR EAST[1]

In discussions of U.S. productivity performance, the Japanese experience is invariably held up as an example to be emulated. But Japan is not the only spectacular success story. At least four other Far Eastern economies—Hong Kong, Singapore, South Korea, and Taiwan—have achieved extraordinary postwar economic records that have hardly been approached elsewhere in the world.

It may, therefore, be interesting to see what policy measures these economies have adopted that may have helped to stimulate their productivity. In examining these measures, we deliberately ignore such influences as work ethic and cultural background because, even if they turn out to be extremely significant, they are not easily transferable and are therefore of limited use as guides for U.S. policy. There are other reasons why we do not intend these economies to be taken as role models. The totalitarian regimes in some of them, the lack of protection of human life in others, and the poor housing conditions in still others are hardly attractive features to be imitated.

One conclusion that seems to emerge immediately from a study of these five Far Eastern "miracle economies" is that neither a democratic nor

---

1. This material was prepared as a background paper for subcommittee discussion and is included as supplementary information. CED's Research and Policy Committee votes to approve only the body of the policy statement; thus, no committee recommendations are contained in this appendix.

Additional background papers dealing with other aspects of the productivity problem will be published in *Stimulation of U.S. Productivity Growth*, edited by William J. Baumol and Kenneth McLennan (forthcoming).

an authoritarian government is a requisite for economic growth. Certainly, growth has occurred both in the very free societies of Japan and Hong Kong and under the authoritarian regime of South Korea. Economies and their productivity are apparently able to grow regardless of whether the press is free, whether the government is elected democratically, or whether the civil liberties of individuals are protected. Authoritarianism and central economic planning are often equated, but in fact the two do not always go together. Political liberty is not restricted in France, but a great deal of government effort has been devoted to planning especially in the large public-sector part of the economy, even before the recent socialist victory at the polls. On the other hand, Hungary and Yugoslavia can hardly be described as democracies, yet their economies have moved far from the Soviet pattern of central direction. Even under the totalitarian regimes of Hitler and Mussolini, business activity was far less constrained by central direction than it is in the Soviet Union and China.

The five Far Eastern economies encompass a broad range of degrees of central planning. In Hong Kong, virtually anything goes as far as business activity is concerned. The Japanese government, on the other hand, plays a significant role in planning the direction of business investment and other aspects of the economy. It takes measures to discourage investment in industries that it believes offer little scope for future growth and seeks to attract investment in those activities that promise the greatest opportunities for expansion and international competitiveness. At the same time, however, it protects its inefficient agriculture from lower-priced imports.

There are at least five pertinent areas in which some of the differences between the Far Eastern growth economies and the U.S. economy may be instructive for American policy. They are:

- labor relations;

- consumer credit, pension and housing arrangements;

- taxation of savings;

- government-directed investment and the regulation of business activity; and

- taxation of business.

In general, no uniform set of policies or approaches is used in all five countries. In fact, in several policy areas, the institutional arrangements differ markedly from one country to another. It follows that there is no unique path to productivity growth, no single prescription whose violation condemns an economy to inferior performance.

Perhaps the clearest conclusion that emerges from the evidence is the importance of eliminating impediments to saving and investment. The most obvious difference between arrangements in the United States and those in the Far Eastern economies is the lack of incentives to consumer borrowing and spending in the Far East and their more liberal treatment—especially tax treatment—of saving and investment. The significance of this is strengthened considerably by a remarkable statistical study of the differences between the productivity performances of the United States and Japan.[2] The study indicates that perhaps *the* major reason for superior Japanese growth is the far more rapid expansion of its capital stock. This expansion has increased the productive capacity of Japanese workers directly and has provided them with the most modern types of plant and equipment.

LABOR RELATIONS

A great deal has been made of the special relationship between management and labor in Japan. The widespread practice of granting workers tenure in their jobs, the use of quality circles, the smaller disparities in wages between workers and management, the greater loyalty of employees to their companies, and the far greater care typically exercised in the selection of the Japanese work force have all been widely noted. But most of the evidence seems to suggest that it is not the particular mechanism of these arrangements that produces such admirable results; mere formal introduction of similar practices in the United States would probably contribute relatively little to productivity growth. There may, however, be different ways to achieve similar results in the United States. Part of the secret of Japanese "miracle management" may lie in the fact that workers in Japan are given a direct stake in the future of the firm, that management has a direct stake in the morale of the labor force, and that both groups are well aware of this reciprocal relationship.

Some reports on the extent and character of these institutional arrangements tend to exaggerate matters. For example, employment tenure seems to be granted to well under half of the Japanese labor force, and companies generally employ large numbers of "temporary" workers whose employ-

---

2. J. R. Norsworthy, testimony on Recent Productivity Trends in the U.S. and Japan before the Subcommittee on Employment and Productivity (97th Congress, 2nd session, 2 April 1982).

ment can readily be terminated. Thus, it is more likely that the much-publicized Japanese employment security is not very different from the sort of job security that many U.S. workers enjoy when they acquire sufficient seniority or, rather, that the difference lies largely in the spirit in which the job security is administered.

Moreover, such special labor-management relationships are not a prevailing characteristic of the other prosperous economies in the Far East. Hong Kong, with its extreme laissez-faire economy, seems to be a clear case in point. There, much economic activity is apparently carried out in what we would regard as sweatshops, where there is nothing akin to job tenure, quality circles, or anything of the sort.

Taiwan also has no permanent employment security system, but because of the rapid growth of its firms, job security has been available de facto; most employees keep their jobs permanently. There is no right to strike, there are no militant labor organizations, and the role of trade unions is minimal. The wage structure, however, provides a great many fringe benefits, including subsidized meals, work uniforms, and dormitories, in lieu of large increases in salaries.

In Hong Kong, the relationship of employers to workers tends to be old-style authoritarian paternalism. This is particularly true of smaller enterprises (which usually provide workers with meals and lodging of some sort), but it is also true of the larger, more modern-minded companies. Larger firms provide many benefits to their workers: subsidized food and meals, housing (especially dormitories for single workers), medical services, transportation to and from work, recreation facilities and other amenities, and substantial bonuses. Hong Kong's workers have the freedom to strike, but unions are a negligible force in the economy.

In Singapore, as in Hong Kong, a high proportion of businesses are family enterprises, and tend to have a markedly paternalistic, authoritarian relationship to their employees. However, unions are larger and more influential than those in Hong Kong, resembling those in Western Europe and North America. The Singapore government actively regulates labor-management relations and controls the rate of wage increases and other labor costs.

The South Korean labor movement has a negligible influence in the economy. There are few powerful organized unions, and labor strikes are prohibited. The docility of the labor force has been secured to a large extent by a great deal of political repression. The Korean system of industrial organization is in many ways similar to the Japanese, with employees tending to remain at one firm for life, loyal to their paternalistic employers.

CONSUMER CREDIT, PENSION, AND HOUSING ARRANGEMENTS

The extraordinarily low rates of saving and of investment in industrial activity in the United States have been attributed to a variety of influences. Two influences that are frequently blamed are the uniquely efficient credit arrangements available to American consumers and the strong tax incentives for investment in non-income-producing private housing. Easy credit, in general, encourages consumption and induces negative savings, both of which use up resources that might otherwise have been devoted to the creation of plant and equipment. The existence of housing subsidies means that, of the relatively meager savings available, a high proportion will be lured into home building rather than into capital equipment for industry. Nothing in any of the five Far Eastern economies corresponds to either U.S. credit arrangements or U.S. incentives for private housing, although governmentally provided housing is not uncommon.

In Japan, there are far fewer old-age benefits and pension programs than there are in the United States; consequently, people are *forced* to save more than Americans do. Families benefit from none of the tax favors for home buying that prevail in the United States, and down payments are typically at least 50 percent. Japanese consumer-credit institutions are generally underdeveloped, and the mortgage market is inadequate; a relatively small portion of Japan's large flow of savings has been made available through credit markets to consumers and homeowners.

The financial resources accounted for by the household sector (consumer credit and home mortgages) in Japan amounted to about 25 to 30 percent of personal disposable income in 1972, and rose to about 58 percent in 1979.[3] In contrast, in the United States, the corresponding ratio of consumer credit (23 percent) and mortgage credit (62 percent) to disposable income remained relatively stable during most of the 1970s and was equal to about 84 percent in 1979. Along with Japan's low ratio of government expenditures to GNP, the limited availability of consumer credit and

---

3. These data for Japan are based on the flow-of-funds accounts, rather than individual statistical series on consumer credit and housing credit. The sum of the two separate series on consumer and housing credit are substantially smaller than the financial liabilities of the Japanese household sector shown in the flow-of-funds accounts. Although the Japanese data derived from the flow-of-funds accounts do not show any breakdown between consumer loans and home mortgages, they are more comparable to those for the U.S. shown above. See Statistical Bureau, Japanese Prime Minister's Office, *Japanese Statistical Yearbook* (Tokyo: Prime Minister's Office, 1972 to 1979).

EMORY & HENRY LIBRARY

home financing has encouraged the flow of the country's savings into business investment.

The supply of credit in Taiwan has been consistently tight despite relatively high interest rates. Government support of social, health, pension, and housing benefits is very limited. The family is the strategic social unit that takes care of these needs. A comparatively small fraction of GNP is devoted to investment in housing (only 2.9 percent in 1974), and housing construction is hampered by high land prices and the difficulty of securing loans. Some private businesses offer housing to employees, mainly dormitories for single workers. Public enterprises provide more extensive housing benefits; for example, the tobacco industry provides fifteen-year, 4-percent loans for up to 40 percent of the cost of a house for its employees, and some government employees can get twenty-year mortgages at 3-percent subsidized interest rates. Some educational subsidies are provided by companies to their employees, but there are no state or private pension plans, nor is there unemployment insurance. Short-term credit mechanisms are not well developed; the postdated check is the main credit instrument.

Over 46 percent of the population of Hong Kong and nearly 40 percent of the population of Singapore live in low-rent government or government-assisted housing. It is expected that by the early 1980s, 65 to 70 percent of the population of Singapore will live in subsidized government-built housing. About two-thirds of these units are rentals, and the remainder are owner-occupied. In recent years, the government has encouraged people to use their mandatory savings contributions to the Central Provident Fund to purchase the housing units on an installment basis.

In South Korea, many companies provide dormitories for unmarried workers and subsidized apartments for married workers. Consumer credit of the sort available in the United States is unknown. For example, in order to buy a house, a family must usually pay the entire amount outright. There is an almost complete lack of mortgage funds, and consumer loans from commercial banks are virtually nonexistent. People rely on savings or loans from family, friends, and business proprietors; and although there is a large, informal "curb" market for loans, the loan period is sharply limited, and interest rates are very high. The housing shortage in Korea is severe, and the government has made little attempt to move financial resources, public or private, into housing. Korean economic policy has channeled the greatest possible investment into the industrial sector. Government support of social services is also very limited in Korea; in 1975, social-benefit outlays were between 4 and 5 percent of total government expenditures, compared with 30 to 40 percent in many advanced industrial countries.

TAXATION AND SAVING

The Japanese save about 22 percent of their disposable income compared to the American rate of only 5 percent. Japan's government uses powerful incentives to promote personal savings: exemption from taxes on smaller amounts of property income and lower rates of tax on property income in general; exemption from taxes on interest income from savings deposits; availability of government bonds; and postal savings (with some limitation on principal values). The income tax law also permits preferential tax rates of 35 percent on interest and dividends.[4] Capital gains from the sale of land or buildings are taxed separately at a lower rate, 20 percent, and capital gains from the sale of securities are tax-exempt. Some benefits in the form of tax credits on savings are accumulated specifically for the purpose of home purchases, thus constituting another form of housing subsidy.

Since the 1950s, fiscal policy in Taiwan has encouraged and enforced rising ratios of savings and has stimulated investment. There has been very little concern about distribution of income. Private household savings are relatively high because of the lack of extensive social programs to underwrite personal risk and the costs of aging. Government tax policy is very generous toward private savings and capital formation. Average tax rates are very low, and there are also specific tax rebates and exemptions that favor savings by private individuals, firms, and corporations. Most households do not pay personal income taxes. Income-tax rates are moderate except in the case of high incomes (with a maximum tax of 60 percent), but even these high rates are mainly theoretical because there are many loopholes and tax evasion is widespread.

In Hong Kong, taxes are very low in general; the income-tax rate, for example, is 17 percent. In Singapore, there are generous incentives to stimulate local and foreign investment; personal income taxes range from 6 to 55 percent, with most families paying little or no income taxes. Both Hong Kong and Singapore rely heavily on domestic savings to fuel investment—Hong Kong through the private sector and Singapore through both the private sector and a large-scale mandatory-saving plan operated by the government. In both Hong Kong and Singapore, credit markets for new enterprises are underdeveloped; entrepreneurs must rely on their own savings and those of family and friends.

---

4. Tax Bureau, Japanese Ministry of Finance, *An Outline of Japanese Taxes, 1981* (Tokyo: Ministry of Finance, 1981).

In South Korea, special tax rates have been devised to foster saving and investment. Currently, interest income from banks is taxed at only 5 percent, and interest from government bonds and from certain corporate issues is not taxable. Certain types of dividend income are subject to a withholding-tax rate of only 5 percent (compared with the general withholding rate of 25 percent) and employee bonuses, up to a certain amount, are exempt from tax.

GOVERNMENT-DIRECTED INVESTMENT

The role of government in guiding industrial investment varies enormously among the prosperous Far Eastern economies. Once again, Hong Kong and Japan provide the greatest contrast. In Hong Kong, industry is left almost entirely free to choose the direction in which it invests its capital. Entrepreneurs select their lines of endeavor and decide when and whether to change them, virtually without impediment or even advice from government. On the other hand, in Japan, as in France (at least until recently), government has for some time considered it part of its role to guide private industrial behavior toward the investment opportunities it determines are most promising for the general welfare.

Although its influence on business has declined significantly in recent years, the Japanese government seeks to guide and encourage industries that are expected to become increasingly competitive internationally. This is done principally through the Ministry of International Trade and Industry (MITI), the Ministry of Finance (MOF), and the Bank of Japan. The government arranges for high-priority industries to get foreign capital, grants choice locations on reclaimed land, gives permission to build new plants, creates tax advantages for companies that modernize their plants, and raises licensing standards to force modernization (if a company cannot meet the standards, it is forced to close down). MITI is able to obtain compliance with its decisions because of its very close, mutually supportive relationship with the business community and its ability to make life difficult for uncooperative companies in such matters as licensing, permits for new plants, approval of support facilities for new plants; major banks may be reluctant to lend money to projects that MITI does not favor. MITI provides guidance on structural modernization of plant and equipment and promotes mergers of companies that lack the capital to implement modernization; it assists companies in declining industries in merging or going out of business while encouraging new ones to move into the same localities and employ the laid-off personnel. Sometimes, it will work out a *depression cartel*, which is an agreement among companies in a depressed sector to reduce production capacity, with the cutbacks distributed relatively evenly among companies.

MITI actually has very little *legal* authority. It can reserve licensing for companies that meet certain standards, must approve new plants that will pollute, can form depression and modernization cartels, control some research expenditures, and grant approval of licensing agreements to companies that affiliate with foreign companies. But the success of MITI depends primarily on the voluntary cooperation of the business community, not on statutory rules. MITI bureaucrats and company officials meet frequently and informally to arrive at mutual understandings, and it is generally true that MITI and the Japanese bureaucracy seek to *stimulate* business rather than regulate and control it. It is worth noting that MITI's decisions have not been mistake-free. In the cases of automobiles, motorcycles, radios, and television sets, some of postwar Japan's most successful product lines, MITI was not a powerful encouraging force; indeed, it took some steps that could be interpreted as discouraging.

All the other rapidly growing Far Eastern economies are highly capitalistic, with very limited public ownership of production. In Taiwan, for example, the scope of government control over the economy has been greatly reduced since the 1950s to produce the existing relatively free-market, free-enterprise system. In Hong Kong, the government has relied almost completely on private initiative and the market process to run the economy. There is complete freedom of trade and capital movement, there is no central bank, and the government does not carry out a policy of macroeconomic management. It relies on market forces to keep production costs and export prices competitive and to reallocate capital and labor continuously into those activities that yield the best returns.

Singapore's government, unlike that of Hong Kong, participates actively in the workings of its economy. It constrains and supplements the operation of market forces by various macroeconomic management policies; it offers tax exemptions, loans, and other incentives to local and foreign enterprises to establish desired industries; and it provides tariff and quota protection to the noncompetitive industries that are regarded as necessary.

The South Korean economy is highly managed, with varying degrees of government control over trade, banks, foreign loan approval, and agricultural-price supports, plus a large amount of direct investment. Heavy export promotion employs various tax exemptions, preferential loans, subsidized inputs, import entitlements, and wastage allowances. Korea's approach to economic growth, like Japan's, stresses technology, export promotion, systems of trade and foreign-exchange controls, and close cooperation between the public and private sectors. In Korea, however, the government-business partnership is very much an unequal one, with government setting the policies and business carrying them out. The government's strongest weapon, control over credit, can be used to put companies out of business. It can also be used to keep companies out of some fields or force them into others through control of funds for expansion. In terms of "non-productive" government regulations, South Korea's industry is largely unfettered. Korean workers, on the average, have the world's longest workweek, almost fifty-four hours for women and fifty-three hours for men. Compared with Japan or the United States, Korea has a very high rate of industrial accidents. Similarly, in Taiwan, government inspection of factories is lax; between 1976 and 1980, Taiwan had the highest rate of workers killed in factory accidents anywhere in the world.

A final difference between the U.S. and other countries is the government's defense policy. Military spending is thought to divert resources for investment for U.S. capital markets in a way that reduces our potential for productivity growth. To the extent that this is true, the U.S. is at a relative disadvantage to some of its competitors who spend a much lower proportion of their GNP on defense.[5]

TAXATION OF BUSINESS AND CAPITAL GAINS

The total tax burden in Japan, although it has risen substantially since the mid-1970s, is still moderate when compared with that in other industrialized countries. The ratio of total tax receipts to gross domestic product in 1980 was 26 percent for Japan, 31 percent for the United States, and 37 percent for Germany.[6] Japan's relatively low tax burden may be attributed partly to the low level of defense expenditures. But it also reflects the fiscal conservatism of the Japanese government in restraining the growth of government expenditures relative to the growth of the economy as a whole.

---

5. Here, experience in the Far Eastern economies is mixed. For example, in the late 1970s, military expenditures in Japan were less than one percent of GNP; but in South Korea, they were over 6 percent. In Taiwan, the defense budget averaged 9 to 11 percent of GNP between 1951 and 1965, accounting for about 85 percent of the combined outlays of government at all levels.

---

6. Organization for Economic Cooperation and Development, *Long-Term Trends in Tax Revenues of OECD Member Countries, 1966–1980* (Paris: Organization for Economic Cooperation and Development, 1981).

The Japanese use tax incentives as a method of stimulating desirable business activity. Like other industrialized countries, Japan has adopted a variety of tax-incentive measures, including accelerated depreciation allowances (which are more favorable than those in other industrialized countries), investment tax credits, and tax-free reserves. In particular, Japan offers substantial incentives for research and development, such as low tax rates and faster depreciation and write-offs for investment in plant and equipment. The Japanese government provides tax credits for incremental R&D expenditures, permits immediate expensing or amortization of all such outlays, and offers tax advantages to small firms for research and development.

The Japanese policy on business taxation has undergone significant change over the past decade. In recent years, the tax-incentive measures to promote business investment in general have been curtailed significantly. In today's context, perhaps the most important feature of the Japanese tax system affecting its business sector is the relatively low tax burden it imposes on the economy as a whole.

In Taiwan, a very generous tax policy encourages capital formation. Rates are very low, and there are many rebates and exemptions. Business income taxes are low but progressive, and, as mentioned previously, there is much tax evasion. Some other elements of the favorable tax climate include the deduction of 2 percent of total export revenue from taxable income, a five-year tax holiday for new firms, tax reduction in the form of accelerated depreciation of fixed assets for established enterprises and for firms increasing their capital for expansion, deductibility of retained earnings used for investment, exemption from income tax of dividends from some firms' new investment, tax rebates for raw materials used to manufacture export goods, and tax exemptions for interest on certain kinds of savings deposits.

Hong Kong has very low rates of taxation. Business profits are taxed at a flat 17 percent (and those profits are exempt from further taxation when they are paid out as dividends), and there are no import or export duties. In Singapore, company profits are taxed at a flat rate of 40 percent.

The South Korean government uses a variety of tax preferences and credit subsidies to promote exports and industrial development. The tax preferences given to the business sector are concentrated among the industries that the government intends to promote. These measures include duty-free access to imported materials and capital goods, preferential depreciation allowances, and credit subsidies.

CONCLUSIONS

In summary, there is no one road to productivity growth. It may occur under democratic or undemocratic regimes. It is compatible with small military outlays and with large ones. It can be achieved through diverse policies and institutional arrangements. The one firm lesson to be learned from the Far Eastern successes is the importance of the removal of disincentives to saving and investment; in this area, all five economies have adopted policies that are very similar and that differ markedly from our own.

In evaluating information of the sort provided here, it it important to note that successful foreign economies are not models to be followed slavishly and that it should not be assumed that foreign successes can continue indefinitely. For example, the extraordinary economic success in Germany following World War II has faded in comparison with the performance of some of its most vigorous competitors. That experience serves as a warning against projections of international competitive relationships and trends far into the future.

It is essential also to reemphasize that the growth rates of the countries described here do not mean that we will want to imitate all or even any of their policies. Many of their arrangements conflict with our standards of freedom or public welfare and are hardly likely to prove attractive to us. This survey has simply sought to provide a dispassionate description of the pertinent facts, not a set of prescriptions for policy.

OBJECTIVES OF THE COMMITTEE FOR ECONOMIC DEVELOPMENT

For over forty years, the Committee for Economic Development has been a respected influence on the formation of business and public policy. CED is devoted to these two objectives:

To develop, through objective research and informed discussion, findings and recommendations for private and public policy that will contribute to preserving and strengthening our free society, achieving steady economic growth at high employment and reasonably stable prices, increasing productivity and living standards, providing greater and more equal opportunity for every citizen, and improving the quality of life for all.

To bring about increasing understanding by present and future leaders in business, government, and education, and among concerned citizens, of the importance of these objectives and the ways in which they can be achieved.

CED's work is supported strictly by private voluntary contributions from business and industry, foundations, and individuals. It is independent, nonprofit, nonpartisan, and nonpolitical.

The two hundred trustees, who generally are presidents or board chairmen of corporations and presidents of universities, are chosen for their individual capacities rather than as representatives of any particular interests. By working with scholars, they unite business judgment and experience with scholarship in analyzing the issues and developing recommendations to resolve the economic problems that constantly arise in a dynamic and democratic society.

Through this business-academic partnership, CED endeavors to develop policy statements and other research materials that commend themselves as guides to public and business policy; that can be used as texts in college economics and political science courses and in management training courses; that will be considered and discussed by newspaper and magazine editors, columnists, and commentators; and that are distributed abroad to promote better understanding of the American economic system.

CED believes that by enabling businessmen to demonstrate constructively their concern for the general welfare, it is helping business to earn and maintain the national and community respect essential to the successful functioning of the free enterprise capitalist system.

CED BOARD OF TRUSTEES

Chairman
FLETCHER L. BYROM, Retired Chairman
Koppers Company, Inc.

Vice Chairmen
OWEN B. BUTLER, Chairman
The Procter & Gamble Company

WILLIAM S. CASHEL, JR., Vice Chairman
American Telephone and Telegraph Company

FRANKLIN A. LINDSAY, Chairman, Executive
    Committee
Itek Corporation

J. PAUL LYET, Former Chairman
Sperry Corporation

WILLIAM F. MAY, Dean
New York University Graduate School
    of Business Administration

RICHARD R. SHINN, Former Chairman
Metropolitan Life Insurance Company

Treasurer
CHARLES J. SCANLON
Essex, Connecticut

A. ROBERT ABBOUD, President
Occidental Petroleum Corporation

RAY C. ADAM, Chairman
NL Industries, Inc.

WILLIAM M. AGEE, Chairman
The Bendix Corporation

RAND V. ARASKOG, Chairman and President
ITT Corporation

ROY L. ASH
Los Angeles, California

RALPH E. BAILEY, Chairman
Conoco Inc.

ROBERT H. B. BALDWIN, Chairman
Morgan Stanley & Co. Incorporated

JOSEPH W. BARR, Corporate Director
Arlington, Virginia

HARRY HOOD BASSETT, Chairman, Executive
    Committee
Southeast Bank N.A.

WARREN L. BATTS, President
Dart & Kraft, Inc.

ROBERT A. BECK, Chairman
The Prudential Insurance Company of America

JACK F. BENNETT, Senior Vice President
Exxon Corporation

JAMES F. BERÉ, Chairman
Borg-Warner Corporation

DAVID BERETTA, Director
Uniroyal, Inc.

DEREK C. BOK, President
Harvard University

ALAN S. BOYD, President
Airbus Industrie of North America

ANDREW F. BRIMMER, President
Brimmer & Company, Inc.

ALFRED BRITTAIN III, Chairman
Bankers Trust Company

JOHN H. BRYAN, JR., Chairman
Consolidated Foods Corporation

THEODORE A. BURTIS, Chairman
Sun Company

OWEN B. BUTLER, Chairman
The Procter & Gamble Company

FLETCHER L. BYROM, Retired Chairman
Koppers Company, Inc.

ALEXANDER CALDER, JR., Chairman
Union Camp Corporation

PHILIP CALDWELL, Chairman
Ford Motor Company

ROBERT J. CARLSON, Executive Vice
    President–Power
United Technologies Corporation

RAFAEL CARRION, JR., Chairman
Banco Popular de Puerto Rico

FRANK T. CARY, Chairman
IBM Corporation

WILLIAM S. CASHEL, JR., Vice Chairman
American Telephone and Telegraph Company

FINN M. W. CASPERSEN, Chairman
Beneficial Corporation

JOHN B. CAVE, Executive Vice President and
    Chief Financial Officer
McGraw-Hill, Inc.

HUGH M. CHAPMAN, Chairman
Citizens & Southern National Bank of South Carolina

ROBERT A. CHARPIE, President
Cabot Corporation

ROBERT CIZIK, President
Cooper Industries, Inc.

DAVID R. CLARE, President
Johnson & Johnson

W. GRAHAM CLAYTOR, JR., President
Amtrak

WILLIAM T. COLEMAN, JR., Senior Partner
O'Melveny & Meyers

*EMILIO G. COLLADO, Chairman
Grace Geothermal Corporation

RICHARD M. CYERT, President
Carnegie-Mellon University

D. RONALD DANIEL, Managing Director
McKinsey & Company, Inc.

JOHN H. DANIELS, Retired Chairman
National City Bancorporation

RONALD R. DAVENPORT, Chairman
Sheridan Broadcasting Corporation

RALPH P. DAVIDSON, Chairman
Time Inc.

J. HALLAM DAWSON, President
Crocker National Bank

WILLIAM N. DERAMUS III, Chairman
Kansas City Southern Industries, Inc.

PETER A. DEROW, President
CBS/Publishing Group

*Life Trustee

JOHN DIEBOLD, Chairman
The Diebold Group, Inc.

ROBERT R. DOCKSON, Chairman
California Federal Savings and Loan Association

EDWIN D. DODD, Chairman
Owens-Illinois, Inc.

DONALD J. DONAHUE, Vice Chairman and
    Operating Officer
Continental Group, Inc.

JOHN T. DORRANCE, JR., Chairman
Campbell Soup Company

JOSEPH P. DOWNER, Vice Chairman
Atlantic Richfield Company

FRANK P. DOYLE, Senior Vice President—Corporate
    Relations Staff
General Electric Company

VIRGINIA A. DWYER, Vice President and Treasurer
American Telephone and Telegraph Company

W. D. EBERLE, President
Manchester Associates, Ltd.

WILLIAM S. EDGERLY, Chairman and President
State Street Bank and Trust Company

JOHN R. EDMAN, Vice President
General Motors Corporation

ROBERT F. ERBURU, President
The Times Mirror Company

THOMAS J. EYERMAN, Partner
Skidmore, Owings & Merrill

WALTER A. FALLON, Chairman
Eastman Kodak Company

JAMES B. FARLEY, Chairman
Booz·Allen & Hamilton Inc.

DAVID C. FARRELL, President
The May Department Stores Company

FRANCIS E. FERGUSON, Chairman
Northwestern Mutual Life Insurance Company

JOHN T. FEY, Chairman
National Bank of North America

JOHN H. FILER, Chairman
Aetna Life and Casualty Company

WILLIAM S. FISHMAN, Chairman
ARA Services, Inc.

EDMUND B. FITZGERALD, President
Northern Telecom Limited

JOSEPH B. FLAVIN, Chairman
The Singer Company

*WILLIAM H. FRANKLIN, Chairman (Retired)
Caterpillar Tractor Co.

ROBERT E. FRAZER, Chairman
Dayton Power & Light Company

DON C. FRISBEE, Chairman
Pacific Power & Light Company

THOMAS J. GALLIGAN, JR., Chairman
Boston Edison Company

DONALD E. GARRETSON, Vice President, Finance
3M Company

CLIFTON C. GARVIN, JR., Chairman
Exxon Corporation

RICHARD L. GELB, Chairman
Bristol-Myers Company

W. H. KROME GEORGE, Chairman
Aluminum Company of America

THOMAS C. GRAHAM, President
Jones & Laughlin Steel Corporation

HARRY J. GRAY, Chairman
United Technologies Corporation

JOHN D. GRAY, Chairman Emeritus
Hart Schaffner & Marx

WILLIAM C. GREENOUGH, Retired Chairman
TIAA and CREF

W. GRANT GREGORY, Chairman
Touche Ross & Co.

DAVID L. GROVE, President
U.S. Council for International Business

RICHARD W. HANSELMAN, President
Genesco Inc.

ROBERT A. HANSON, Chairman and President
Deere & Company

JOHN D. HARPER, Retired Chairman
Aluminum Company of America

FRED L. HARTLEY, Chairman and President
Union Oil Company of California

BARBARA B. HAUPTFUHRER, Corporate Director
Huntingdon Valley, Pennsylvania

ARTHUR HAUSPURG, Chairman
Consolidated Edison Company

PHILIP M. HAWLEY, President
Carter Hawley Hale Stores, Inc.

HAROLD W. HAYNES, Executive Vice President
    and Chief Financial Officer
The Boeing Company

LAWRENCE HICKEY, Chairman
Stein Roe & Farnham

RODERICK M. HILLS, Chairman
Sears World Trade, Inc.

WAYNE M. HOFFMAN, Chairman
Tiger International, Inc.

ROBERT C. HOLLAND, President
Committee for Economic Development

LEON C. HOLT, JR., Vice Chairman
Air Products and Chemicals, Inc.

ROY M. HUFFINGTON, President
Roy M. Huffington, Inc.

GORDON C. HURLBERT, President—Power
    Systems Company
Westinghouse Electric Corporation

FREDERICK G. JAICKS, Chairman
Inland Steel Company

HARRY J. KANE, Executive Vice President
Georgia-Pacific Corporation

DAVID T. KEARNS, President
Xerox Corporation

GEORGE M. KELLER, Chairman
Standard Oil Company of California

DONALD P. KELLY, Chairman and President
Esmark, Inc.

J. C. KENEFICK, Chairman
Union Pacific Railroad Company

JAMES L. KETELSEN, Chairman
Tenneco Inc.

TOM KILLEFER, Chairman, Executive Committee
United States Trust Company of New York

E. ROBERT KINNEY, President
Investors Group of Companies

*Life Trustee

PHILIP M. KLUTZNICK, Senior Partner
Klutznick Investments

RALPH LAZARUS, Chairman, Executive Committee
Federated Department Stores, Inc.

JAMES E. LEE, Chairman
Gulf Oil Corporation

FLOYD W. LEWIS, Chairman and President
Middle South Utilities, Inc.

FRANKLIN A. LINDSAY, Chairman,
    Executive Committee
Itek Corporation

JOHN A. LOVE, Chairman and President
Ideal Basic Industries

GEORGE M. LOW, President
Rensselaer Polytechnic Institute

FRANCIS P. LUCIER, Chairman
The Black & Decker Manufacturing Company

ROBERT W. LUNDEEN, Chairman
The Dow Chemical Company, Inc.

J. PAUL LYET, Former Chairman
Sperry Corporation

BRUCE K. MacLAURY, President
The Brookings Institution

MALCOLM MacNAUGHTON, Chairman,
    Executive Committee
Castle & Cooke, Inc.

G. BARRON MALLORY
New York, New York

WILLIAM A. MARQUARD, Chairman
American Standard Inc.

WILLIAM F. MAY, Dean
New York University Graduate School
    of Business Administration

JEAN MAYER, President
Tufts University

ALONZO L. McDONALD, Consultant
Bloomfield Hills, Michigan

JOHN F. McGILLICUDDY, Chairman
Manufacturers Hanover Corporation

JAMES W. McKEE, JR., Chairman
CPC International Inc.

JOHN A. McKINNEY, Chairman
Manville Corporation

CHAMPNEY A. McNAIR, Vice Chairman
Trust Company of Georgia

E. L. McNEELY
La Jolla, California

J. W. McSWINEY, Director
The Mead Corporation

ROBERT E. MERCER, Vice Chairman
The Goodyear Tire & Rubber Company

RUBEN F. METTLER, Chairman
TRW Inc.

T. JUSTIN MOORE, JR., Chairman
Virginia Electric and Power Company

LEE L. MORGAN, Chairman
Caterpillar Tractor Co.

STEVEN MULLER, President
The Johns Hopkins University

BARBARA W. NEWELL, Chancellor
State University System of Florida

EDWARD N. NEY, Chairman
Young & Rubicam Inc.

WILLIAM S. OGDEN, Vice Chairman
    and Chief Financial Officer
The Chase Manhattan Bank

ANTHONY J. F. O'REILLY, President
H. J. Heinz Company

NORMA PACE, Senior Vice President
American Paper Institute

THOMAS O. PAINE, President
Thomas Paine Associates

VICTOR H. PALMIERI, Chairman
Victor Palmieri and Company Incorporated

DANIEL PARKER, Honorary Chairman
The Parker Pen Company

JOHN H. PERKINS, President
Continental Illinois National Bank
    and Trust Company of Chicago

S. R. PETERSEN, Chairman
Getty Oil Company

C. WREDE PETERSMEYER
Vero Beach, Florida

MARTHA E. PETERSON, President Emeritus
Beloit College

PETER G. PETERSON, Chairman and President
Lehman Brothers Kuhn Loeb, Inc.

JOHN G. PHILLIPS, Chairman
The Louisiana Land and Exploration Company

DEAN P. PHYPERS, Senior Vice President
IBM Corporation

DONALD C. PLATTEN, Chairman
Chemical Bank

EDMUND T. PRATT, JR., Chairman
Pfizer Inc.

LELAND S. PRUSSIA, Chairman
Bank of America N.T. & S.A.

JOHN R. PURCELL, Chairman
SFN Companies, Inc.

R. STEWART RAUCH, Chairman, Executive Committee
General Accident Insurance Companies

JAMES Q. RIORDAN, Executive Vice President
Mobil Corporation

BRUCE M. ROCKWELL, Chairman
Colorado National Bank

FRANCIS C. ROONEY, JR., Chairman
Melville Corporation

THOMAS F. RUSSELL, Chairman
Federal-Mogul Corporation

JOHN SAGAN, Vice President-Treasurer
Ford Motor Company

RALPH S. SAUL, Chairman
CIGNA Corporation

CHARLES J. SCANLON
Essex, Connecticut

HENRY B. SCHACHT, Chairman
Cummins Engine Company, Inc.

ROBERT M. SCHAEBERLE, Chairman
Nabisco Brands Inc.

J. L. SCOTT, Chairman
J. L. Scott Enterprises, Inc.

D. C. SEARLE, Chairman, Executive Committee
G. D. Searle & Co.

DONALD V. SEIBERT, Chairman
J. C. Penney Company, Inc.

DONNA E. SHALALA, President
Hunter College

MARK SHEPHERD, JR., Chairman
Texas Instruments Incorporated

RICHARD R. SHINN, Former Chairman
Metropolitan Life Insurance Company

ROCCO C. SICILIANO, Chairman
Ticor

ANDREW C. SIGLER, Chairman
Champion International Corporation

WILLIAM P. SIMMONS, Chairman
First National Bank & Trust Company

L. EDWIN SMART, Chairman and President
Trans World Corporation

DONALD B. SMILEY, Chairman, Finance Committee
R. H. Macy & Co., Inc.

PHILIP L. SMITH, President
General Foods Corporation

RICHARD M. SMITH, Vice Chairman
Bethlehem Steel Corporation

ROGER B. SMITH, Chairman
General Motors Corporation

ELMER B. STAATS
Former Comptroller General of the United States
Washington, D.C.

CHARLES B. STAUFFACHER, Financial Consultant
Universe Tank Ships, Inc.

DONALD M. STEWART, President
Spelman College

J. PAUL STICHT, Chairman
R. J. Reynolds Industries, Inc.

GEORGE A. STINSON, Chairman, Executive Committee
National Steel Corporation

WILLIAM P. STIRITZ, Chairman
Ralston Purina Company

*WILLIAM C. STOLK
Easton, Connecticut

WILLIS A. STRAUSS, Chairman
InterNorth, Inc.

BARRY F. SULLIVAN, Chairman
First National Bank of Chicago

G. J. TANKERSLEY, Chairman
Consolidated Natural Gas Company.

DAVID S. TAPPAN, JR., President
Fluor Corporation

EDWARD R. TELLING, Chairman
Sears, Roebuck and Co.

WALTER N. THAYER, Chairman
Whitney Communications Corporation

W. BRUCE THOMAS, Vice Chairman of
Administration and Chief Financial Officer
United States Steel Corporation

G. ROBERT TRUEX, JR., Chairman
Rainier National Bank

L. S. TURNER, JR., Executive Vice President
Texas Utilities Company

THOMAS V. H. VAIL
President, Publisher, and Editor
Plain Dealer Publishing Company

THOMAS A. VANDERSLICE, President
GTE Corporation

ALVIN W. VOGTLE, JR., President
The Southern Company, Inc.

ALVA O. WAY, President
The Travelers Corporation

SIDNEY J. WEINBERG, JR., Partner
Goldman, Sachs & Co.

GEORGE WEISSMAN, Chairman
Philip Morris Incorporated

JOHN F. WELCH, JR., Chairman
General Electric Company

CLIFTON R. WHARTON, JR., Chancellor
State University of New York

ALTON W. WHITEHOUSE, JR., Chairman
Standard Oil Company (Ohio)

*FRAZAR B. WILDE, Chairman Emeritus
Connecticut General Life Insurance Company

HAROLD M. WILLIAMS, President
The J. Paul Getty Museum

J. KELLEY WILLIAMS, President
First Mississippi Corporation

L. STANTON WILLIAMS, Chairman
PPG Industries, Inc.

*W. WALTER WILLIAMS
Seattle, Washington

MARGARET S. WILSON, Chairman
Scarbroughs

RICHARD D. WOOD, Chairman and President
Eli Lilly and Company

WILLIAM S. WOODSIDE, Chairman
American Can Company

*Life Trustee

HONORARY TRUSTEES

E. SHERMAN ADAMS
New Preston, Connecticut

CARL E. ALLEN
North Muskegon, Michigan

JAMES L. ALLEN, Honorary Chairman
Booz·Allen & Hamilton Inc.

O. KELLEY ANDERSON
Boston, Massachusetts

ROBERT O. ANDERSON, Chairman
Atlantic Richfield Company

SANFORD S. ATWOOD
Lake Toxaway, North Carolina

S. CLARK BEISE, President (Retired)
Bank of America N.T. & S.A.

GEORGE F. BENNETT, President
State Street Investment Corporation

HAROLD H. BENNETT
Salt Lake City, Utah

HOWARD W. BLAUVELT, Consultant and Director
Conoco Inc.

JOSEPH L. BLOCK, Former Chairman
Inland Steel Company

ROGER M. BLOUGH
Hawley, Pennsylvania

FRED J. BORCH
New Canaan, Connecticut

MARVIN BOWER, Director
McKinsey & Company, Inc.

R. MANNING BROWN, JR., Director
New York Life Insurance Co., Inc.

JOHN L. BURNS, President
John L. Burns and Company

THOMAS D. CABOT, Honorary Chairman
Cabot Corporation

EDWARD W. CARTER, Chairman
Carter Hawley Hale Stores, Inc.

EVERETT N. CASE
Van Hornesville, New York

HUNG WO CHING, Chairman
Aloha Airlines, Inc.

WALKER L. CISLER
Detroit, Michigan

ROBERT C. COSGROVE
Naples, Florida

GARDNER COWLES, Honorary Chairman
Cowles Communications, Inc.

GEORGE S. CRAFT
Atlanta, Georgia

JOHN P. CUNNINGHAM
Honorary Chairman
Cunningham & Walsh, Inc.

ARCHIE K. DAVIS, Chairman (Retired)
Wachovia Bank and Trust Company, N.A.

DONALD C. DAYTON, Director
Dayton Hudson Corporation

DOUGLAS DILLON, Chairman, Executive Committee
Dillon, Read and Co. Inc.

ALFRED W. EAMES, JR., Director
Del Monte Corporation

ROBERT W. ELSASSER
Management and Economic Consultant
New Orleans, Louisiana

EDMUND FITZGERALD
Milwaukee, Wisconsin

WILLIAM C. FOSTER
Washington, D.C.

JOHN M. FOX
Florida National Investors, Inc.

CLARENCE FRANCIS
New York, New York

DAVID L. FRANCIS, Chairman
Princess Coals, Inc.

GAYLORD FREEMAN
Chicago, Illinois

PAUL S. GEROT, Honorary Chairman
The Pillsbury Company

CARL J. GILBERT
Dover, Massachusetts

KATHARINE GRAHAM, Chairman
The Washington Post Company

WALTER A. HAAS, JR., Honorary Chairman
Levi Strauss and Co.

MICHAEL L. HAIDER
New York, New York

TERRANCE HANOLD
Minneapolis, Minnesota

ROBERT S. HATFIELD
New York, New York

H. J. HEINZ II, Chairman
H. J. Heinz Company

J. V. HERD, Director
The Continental Insurance Companies

OVETA CULP HOBBY, Chairman
The Houston Post

GEORGE F. JAMES
South Bristol, Maine

HENRY R. JOHNSTON
Ponte Vedra Beach, Florida

GILBERT E. JONES, Retired Vice Chairman
IBM Corporation

THOMAS ROY JONES
Carmel, California

FREDERICK R. KAPPEL
Sarasota, Florida

CHARLES KELLER, JR.
New Orleans, Louisiana

DAVID M. KENNEDY
Salt Lake City, Utah

JAMES R. KENNEDY
Essex Fells, New Jersey

CHARLES N. KIMBALL, President Emeritus
Midwest Research Institute

HARRY W. KNIGHT, Chairman
Hillsboro Associates, Inc.

SIGURD S. LARMON
New York, New York

ELMER L. LINDSETH
Shaker Heights, Ohio

JAMES A. LINEN
Greenwich, Connecticut

GEORGE H. LOVE
Pittsburgh, Pennsylvania

ROBERT A. LOVETT, Partner
Brown Brothers Harriman & Co.

ROY G. LUCKS
Del Monte Corporation

FRANKLIN J. LUNDING
Boca Grande, Florida

RAY W. MacDONALD, Honorary Chairman
Burroughs Corporation

IAN MacGREGOR, Honorary Chairman
AMAX Inc.

FRANK L. MAGEE
Stahlstown, Pennsylvania

STANLEY MARCUS, Consultant
Carter Hawley Hale Stores, Inc.

JOSEPH A. MARTINO, Honorary Chairman
NL Industries, Inc.

AUGUSTINE R. MARUSI, Chairman, Executive
    Committee
Borden Inc.

OSCAR G. MAYER, Retired Chairman
Oscar Mayer & Co.

L. F. McCOLLUM
Houston, Texas

JOHN A. McCONE
Pebble Beach, California

GEORGE C. McGHEE, Corporate Director
    and former U.S. Ambassador
Washington, D.C.

CHAUNCEY J. MEDBERRY III, Chairman, Executive
    Committee
Bank of America N.T. & S.A.

JOHN F. MERRIAM
San Francisco, California

LORIMER D. MILTON
Citizens Trust Company

DON G. MITCHELL
Summit, New Jersey

ROBERT R. NATHAN, Chairman
Robert R. Nathan Associates, Inc.

ALFRED C. NEAL
Harrison, New York

J. WILSON NEWMAN, Chairman, Finance Committee
Dun & Bradstreet Companies, Inc.

AKSEL NIELSEN, Chairman, Finance Committee
Ladd Petroleum Corporation

EDWIN W. PAULEY, Chairman
Pauley Petroleum, Inc.

MORRIS B. PENDLETON
Vernon, California

HOWARD C. PETERSEN
Philadelphia, Pennsylvania

RUDOLPH A. PETERSON, President (Retired)
Bank of America N.T. & S.A.

PHILIP D. REED
New York, New York

MELVIN J. ROBERTS
Denver, Colorado

AXEL G. ROSIN, Retired Chairman
Book-of-the-Month Club, Inc.

WILLIAM M. ROTH
San Francisco, California

GEORGE RUSSELL
Bloomfield Hills, Michigan

E. C. SAMMONS
Chairman (Emeritus)
The United States National Bank of Oregon

JOHN A. SCHNEIDER, President
Warner Amex Satellite Entertainment Corporation

ELLERY SEDGWICK, JR.
Cleveland Heights, Ohio

ROBERT B. SEMPLE, Retired Chairman
BASF Wyandotte Corporation

LEON SHIMKIN, Chairman
Simon and Schuster, Inc.

NEIL D. SKINNER
Indianapolis, Indiana

ELLIS D. SLATER
Landrum, South Carolina

S. ABBOT SMITH
Boston, Massachusetts

DAVIDSON SOMMERS
Washington, D.C.

ROBERT C. SPRAGUE, Honorary Chairman
Sprague Electric Company

ELVIS J. STAHR, President Emeritus
National Audubon Society

FRANK STANTON
New York, New York

SYDNEY STEIN, JR., Partner
Stein Roe & Farnham

EDGAR B. STERN, JR., President
Royal Street Corporation

ALEXANDER L. STOTT
Fairfield, Connecticut

CHARLES P. TAFT
Cincinnati, Ohio

C. A. TATUM, JR., Chairman
Texas Utilities Company

ALAN H. TEMPLE
New York, New York

WAYNE E. THOMPSON, Chairman
The Hill Health Care Corporation

CHARLES C. TILLINGHAST, JR.
Managing Director, Merrill Lynch
    White Weld Capital Markets Group
Merrill Lynch, Pierce, Fenner & Smith Inc.

HOWARD S. TURNER, Chairman, Executive
    Committee
Turner Construction Company

ROBERT C. WEAVER
New York, New York

JAMES E. WEBB
Washington, D.C.

WILLIAM H. WENDEL, Vice Chairman
Kennecott Corporation

J. HUBER WETENHALL
New York, New York

GEORGE L. WILCOX, Retired Vice Chairman
Westinghouse Electric Corporation

ARTHUR M. WOOD, Director
Sears, Roebuck and Co.

THEODORE O. YNTEMA
Department of Economics
Oakland University

Honorary Trustees On Leave For Government Service

LINCOLN GORDON
National Intelligence Officer-at-Large
Central Intelligence Agency

WILLIAM A. HEWITT
U.S. Ambassador to Jamaica

RESEARCH ADVISORY BOARD

Chairman
EDWIN S. MILLS
Chairman
Department of Economics
Princeton University

WILLIAM J. BAUMOL
Professor of Economics
Princeton University and New
   York University

GARRY D. BREWER
Professor of Political Science
School of Organization and
   Management
Yale University

ALAN K. CAMPBELL
Executive Vice President
Management and Public Affairs
ARA Services, Inc.

RICHARD N. COOPER
Maurits C. Boas Professor of
   International Economics
Harvard University

GLENN C. LOURY
Professor of Economics
   and Afro-American Studies
Harvard University

R. G. PENNER
Resident Scholar
American Enterprise Institute
   for Public Policy Research

THOMAS C. SCHELLING
Professor of Political Economy
John Fitzgerald Kennedy
   School of Government
Harvard University

*CHARLES L. SCHULTZE
Visiting Professor of Research
Graduate School of Business
Stanford University

LEONARD SILK
Economic Affairs Columnist
The New York Times

*on leave from the Brookings Institution

CED PROFESSIONAL AND ADMINISTRATIVE STAFF

ROBERT C. HOLLAND
President

SOL HURWITZ
Senior Vice President and
   Secretary, Board of Trustees

KENNETH McLENNAN
Vice President and Director
   of Industrial Studies

CLAUDIA P. FEUREY
Director of Information

FRANK W. SCHIFF
Vice President
   and Chief Economist

NATHANIEL M. SEMPLE
Vice President,
   Director of Governmental
   Affairs, and Secretary,
   Research and Policy Committee

PATRICIA O'CONNELL
Director of Finance

*S. CHARLES BLEICH
Vice President and Secretary,
   Board of Trustees

R. SCOTT FOSLER
Vice President and
   Director of Government Studies

ELIZABETH J. LUCIER
Comptroller

Research

SEONG H. PARK
Economist

Business-Government Relations

MARGARET J. HERRE
Assistant Director and
   Assistant Secretary,
   Research and Policy Committee

Conferences

RUTH MUNSON
Manager

Information and Publications

HECTOR GUENTHER
Associate Director

SANDRA KESSLER
Assistant Director

H. MAUREEN GRANEY
Publications Manager

HUGH D. STIER, JR.
Information Analyst

TIMOTHY MUENCH
Staff Associate

Finance

RUTH KALLA
Associate Director

PHILIP TORCHIO
Associate Director

AMY JEAN O'NEILL
Campaign Coordinator

*Administrative Assistants
to the President*

THEODORA BOSKOVIC
SHIRLEY R. SHERMAN

*retired December 1982

STATEMENTS ON NATIONAL POLICY
ISSUED BY THE RESEARCH AND POLICY COMMITTEE

SELECTED PUBLICATIONS

Productivity Policy: Key to the Nation's Economic Future *(April 1983)*

Energy Prices and Public Policy *(July 1982)*

Public-Private Partnership: An Opportunity for Urban Communities *(February 1982)*

Reforming Retirement Policies *(September 1981)*

Transnational Corporations and Developing Countries: New Policies for a Changing World Economy *(April 1981)*

Fighting Inflation and Rebuilding a Sound Economy *(September 1980)*

Stimulating Technological Progress *(January 1980)*

Helping Insure Our Energy Future: A Program for Developing Synthetic Fuel Plants Now *(July 1979)*

Redefining Government's Role in the Market System *(July 1979)*

Improving Management of the Public Work Force: The Challenge to State and Local Government *(November 1978)*

Jobs for the Hard-to-Employ: New Directions for a Public-Private Partnership *(January 1978)*

An Approach to Federal Urban Policy *(December 1977)*

Key Elements of a National Energy Strategy *(June 1977)*

The Economy in 1977–78: Strategy for an Enduring Expansion *(December 1976)*

Nuclear Energy and National Security *(September 1976)*

Fighting Inflation and Promoting Growth *(August 1976)*

Improving Productivity in State and Local Government *(March 1976)*

*International Economic Consequences of High-Priced Energy *(September 1975)*

Broadcasting and Cable Television: Policies for Diversity and Change *(April 1975)*

Achieving Energy Independence *(December 1974)*

A New U.S. Farm Policy for Changing World Food Needs *(October 1974)*

Congressional Decision Making for National Security *(September 1974)*

*Toward a New International Economic System: A Joint Japanese-American View *(June 1974)*

More Effective Programs for a Cleaner Environment *(April 1974)*

The Management and Financing of Colleges *(October 1973)*

Strengthening the World Monetary System *(July 1973)*

Financing the Nation's Housing Needs *(April 1973)*

Building a National Health-Care System *(April 1973)*

*A New Trade Policy Toward Communist Countries *(September 1972)*

High Employment Without Inflation:
  A Positive Program for Economic Stabilization *(July 1972)*

Reducing Crime and Assuring Justice *(June 1972)*

Military Manpower and National Security *(February 1972)*

The United States and the European Community:
  Policies for a Changing World Economy *(November 1971)*

Improving Federal Program Performance *(September 1971)*

Social Responsibilities of Business Corporations *(June 1971)*

Education for the Urban Disadvantaged:
  From Preschool to Employment *(March 1971)*

Further Weapons Against Inflation *(November 1970)*

Making Congress More Effective *(September 1970)*

Training and Jobs for the Urban Poor *(July 1970)*

Improving the Public Welfare System *(April 1970)*

Reshaping Government in Metropolitan Areas *(February 1970)*

Economic Growth in the United States *(October 1969)*

Assisting Development in Low-Income Countries *(September 1969)*

*Nontariff Distortions of Trade *(September 1969)*

Fiscal and Monetary Policies for Steady Economic Growth *(January 1969)*

Financing a Better Election System *(December 1968)*

Innovation in Education: New Directions for the American School *(July 1968)*

Modernizing State Government *(July 1967)*

*Trade Policy Toward Low-Income Countries *(June 1967)*

How Low Income Countries Can Advance Their Own Growth *(September 1966)*

Modernizing Local Government *(July 1966)*

Budgeting for National Objectives *(January 1966)*

*Statements issued in association with CED counterpart organizations in foreign countries.

CED COUNTERPART ORGANIZATIONS
IN FOREIGN COUNTRIES

Close relations exist between the Committee for Economic Development and independent, nonpolitical research organizations in other countries. Such counterpart groups are composed of business executives and scholars and have objectives similar to those of CED, which they pursue by similarly objective methods. CED cooperates with these organizations on research and study projects of common interest to the various countries concerned. This program has resulted in a number of joint policy statements involving such international matters as energy, East-West trade, assistance to the developing countries, and the reduction of nontariff barriers to trade.

CE	Círculo de Empresarios *Serrano Jover 5-2°, Madrid 8, Spain*
CEDA	Committee for Economic Development of Australia *139 Macquarie Street, Sydney 2001* *New South Wales, Australia*
CEPES	Europäische Vereinigung für Wirtschaftliche und Soziale Entwicklung *Reuterweg 14, 6000 Frankfurt/Main, West Germany*
IDEP	Institut de l'Entreprise *6, rue Clément-Marot, 75008 Paris, France*
経済同友会	Keizai Doyukai (Japan Committee for Economic Development) *Japan Industrial Club Bldg.* *1 Marunouchi, Chiyoda-ku, Tokyo, Japan*
PSI	Policy Studies Institute *1-2 Castle Lane, London SW1E 6DR, England*
SNS	Studieförbundet Näringsliv och Samhälle *Sköldungagatan 2, 11427 Stockholm, Sweden*

DATE DUE

GAYLORD

PRINTED IN U.S.A.

Emory & Henry College   Kelly Library

3 1836 0005 3866 0